The Public Triumph

Public Relations for the Strong
…and Those Who Want to Be

JAMES M. CHITTENDEN

Produced by Tara Richter www.RichterPublishing.com

Edited by: Casey Cavanagh & Miki West

Book Cover Designed by: Micah Reyes

Copyright © 2014

James M. Chittenden

ISBN: 0615979807
ISBN-13: 9780615979809

TABLE OF CONTENTS

James M. Chittenden

ACKNOWLEDGMENTS

This page is to recognize the contributions of just a few people. This book happened because somewhere along the way, I received an idea or some form of directly related support from you. Your impact is in these pages, and you will always have my gratitude.

Adam Anderson
Lynette Barry
A. Lyn Bell
Colonel Annita Best, USMCR
Michael Bilello
David Buchthal
Mayor Bob Buckhorn, City of Tampa, FL
Charles Burr
Charlie Burr
Councilwoman Yvonne Yolie Capin, City of Tampa, FL
Brigadier General Stephen Cheney, USMC
Edward Chittenden
Harry Chittenden
Olivia Chittenden
Tyson Chittenden
Holly Clifford
Andrea Emery Cumbie
Larry Dawson
Keith Faust
Jeffery Gitomer
Ben Haynes
Tim Henderlong
Ina Hopper
Lane Houk

Major Jason Johnston, USMC
Rob Lakritz
Eddie Lastra
Nikki LeClair
Lieutenant Colonel Richard Long, USMC
Eric Lucero
Norma Gene Lykes
Steve Marotta
Major General Joseph McMenamin, USMC
Keith Milks
Colonel Richard Motl, USMC
Dr. Mike Murdock
Carl Norton
Colonel Keith Oliver, USMC
Major General and Mrs. O.L. Peacock, USA
John Plumley
Eric Polins
Matt Preston
Art Prioletta
Jennifer Radcliff
Bud Reichel
Micah Reyes
Tara Richter
Yvonne St. Cyr
Colonel Bryan Salas, USMC
Tim Shearer
Chris Siciliano
Russell Taylor
Greg Thomas
Ken Tinnin
Colonel Stuart Wagner, USMC
Major Rob Winchester, USMC
Kevin Woodside

INTRODUCTION

The most satisfying experience in public relations is when you get noticed and recognized for your strengths. Your strengths lie in your difference. Your value is derived from your difference.

While the world exacts a price from all of us from time to time for being ourselves, it also rewards us for it. The strong know how to maximize the value of difference. To strong people, difference is much more of an asset than a liability. It is that difference that drives you to launch a new business. You can do something different and better than your competition. The media might be interested.

You may have done this already and are successful. You may be in the process of doing it and looking for success. Or, you may be considering doing it. Either way, there is something for you in this book.

Strong people handle themselves and others in a way that is direct and straightforward, but graceful. That applies to business, to life, and to public relations as well. Strong people realize that they never stop making mistakes, but they improve as a result of them. Those who are not strong do not profit from mistakes because they are too busy denying them, justifying them, or shifting responsibility for them.

The strong run organizations and businesses that handle

problems in a straightforward and effective manner. They don't avoid them. These are the organizations that find that media can be surprisingly friendly and helpful.

If you conduct business that way, the media will give you little trouble. However, the media may become an "enemy" if you are hiding sustained and willful bad practices. Secrets can make it very hard to build or maintain a strong public image.

Public relations cannot turn you into something that you are not. However, it can be a very effective way to establish a public identity that is based on your strengths and your difference.

This book will help you clarify what that strength is. It will help you to learn to recognize difference in yourself, because you can't tell the story of what it is until you can define it. It will also help you to recognize difference in others, and to work with or around those who are NOT strong.

You can't build a strong organization until you can clarify who is really on your side and who will be strong for you and with you.

Then, we will go to boot camp. "We're looking for a few good men". The U.S. Marine Corps recruits and trains thousands of young people each year, making them stronger and more disciplined. They built and sustain a brand that way, and I will show you how that is done. There are case studies in this book from Marine Corps recruit training at Parris Island, S.C., both in how people are handled and media as well. Use the lessons from the case studies to build your own strong brand.

Then, we will improve your writing and public communication skills. You will learn what is considered newsworthy from a reporter's viewpoint so that you can most effectively present stories to them. You will learn how to spot opportunities to gain media attention.

If you are an entrepreneur or business owner, this book will answer questions about measuring the effectiveness of a public relations investment. It will also provide you with a "do it yourself" plan to establish an online presence and a public reputation.

This book has been described as a "public relations boot camp" and as a "business boot camp". That is accurate. Since we are on that subject, boot camp teaches others before self. So, I leave you with this thought.

Put your business first. If personal glory or attention is your sole motive, you will get it but your reputation will reflect it. Pursue publicity to highlight what you can do for others. Use it to highlight the problems you solve. Use it in the service of enhancing your reputation as a resource and your sales, profits and success will follow.

James M. Chittenden

Chapter 1 Begin!

Congratulations on taking the first steps to getting noticed your way, for your strengths. In these pages you will find what it takes to quickly get you there. To publicize yourself right, be yourself.

That is harder than it looks. Many people trade what they really love for security. Doing that is suicide in slow motion.

Maybe you like being part of a group and can adapt well. If you value adapting to a group, fitting in, and security above all else, then maybe you belong in a large corporation or organization.

If on the other hand, you feel that the time is approaching to try things your way, on your terms, you may be right. If you are disciplined, have courage, and want to be measured against nobody's yardstick but your own, you may be at least temperamentally suited for entrepreneurship.

This book has a few tests. These are not the sort of tests you took in school. Instead, they are illustrations. They are intended to make you answer questions you may not realize that you should be asking. They are meant to check agreement between your mind and your instincts.

The "One day I should" test

Fill in this blank: "I have always wanted to____. Maybe someday, I'll get around to doing ____."

The "flash answer" is the very first answer that appears. Right there…what was that?

If you are like most people, you buried that flash answer under some analysis. You second guessed it.

"Well, I don't have the money for that."
"I've got to pay my bills".
"I just don't have time to get started on that."
"You don't understand. I have responsibilities."
"Realistically, I can't."

The flash answer is a clue to what is at your core.

If you are filling your days with activities or people that don't allow you to do what you are meant to do, then change. What are you waiting for?

There are things that you do well, things that you are better at than most people. All of your life, people have told you that you are good at something.

What were you praised for as a child?

What are you praised for now?

Look for similarities between the two answers. That is another clue. The world is trying to tell you something.

You have a purpose. You have an assignment. There is something you are equipped to do, and if you don't orient your life in that direction, you risk eroding your long-term happiness. You can try other careers and find some elements of happiness while doing that. You can pick up skills while doing that. But you have to trust the spirit. Re-establish the connection between the spirit and the mind. When that connection is strong, you do your best thinking.

However, that connection can be clouded. Emotions cloud it. Fatigue clouds it. Stress clouds it. Drugs and alcohol cloud it. Lust clouds it. Greed clouds it. Previous bad experiences cloud it. That is why we make our worst decisions while under the influence of one or more of those things.

If you could clear away all that clouds the pathway between your spirit and your mind, you will find that it comes to you. You will have certainty about what you should do, what problems you are meant to solve and what service you are meant to render. You will get good at it, and that will make you strong.

You may be there now. Either way, keep reading.

The Pre-Kindergarten Test

You had it all figured out before you started kindergarten.

Go back to when you were four years old. Someone asked you what you wanted to be when you grow up. A four year-old boy might say he wants to be a firefighter. A four year-old girl may say that she wants to be a veterinarian.

Neither of those children have any idea what it actually means to be a firefighter or a veterinarian. But those jobs represent something important. It is what it represents that holds the clues.

What you love the most is a clue to your assignment. What you hate is a clue to something you are meant to correct.

What is it that you have always liked to read about? What is it that you always like to learn about in your spare time? What is it that you like to talk about? What do you enjoy hearing about?

What is it that you have natural and effortless wisdom for?

These are the things that make you different. Your difference is why people seek you out. Your difference is why you can solve problems that others cannot. Your difference is what makes you valuable, and your difference is where you find your rewards.

Isolate that difference and turn it into the centerpiece of your professional life.

In the chapters that follow, you will read about being different from the norm and have fun challenging the norm. You will learn how to be known for your difference—to set yourself apart. You will learn how to get things done in spite of the inaction of others. You will learn to uncover your strength and enhance your reputation.

I am going to take you to boot camp. You will be amazed at what you learn there.

I will teach you basic search engine optimization. I will teach you the fundamentals of public relations, and I will teach you how to be a better writer. You will learn about turning public relations into money. At the end, I will give you a do-it-yourself plan to get noticed quickly. Let's begin.

Chapter 2 Ways to Break the Mold

Breaking the Mold, Part 1

"I'm sorry...we are very busy"

In our business culture, we tend to speak in polite code when delivering bad news, rejection, or excuses. We can be eagerly and effortlessly forthright with good news such as telling someone that they are hired, that their project is progressing well, or that you have agreed on price and terms. Yet when the opposite is true, people hide behind gatekeepers, voicemail, e-mail, or whatever else it takes to avoid confrontation. One way that we hide and let each other know that we have not delivered is to talk about how "busy" we are.

"I'm sorry I never got back to you. I've been slammed". "I am too busy to look at this until the end of next week."

"My (or my boss's) plate is full".
"I'm so swamped".

You will rarely hear such talk from the strong. You will hear it often from those who are not. We have all heard this and sometimes it is bovine scatology (more commonly known as BS). In fact, most of us have been guilty of it.

Of course it may be true. You can never be sure of someone else's burdens. Certainly, a valued partner is worthy of the benefit of the doubt from time to time.

However, nobody pays us to talk about our problems or workload. We make our living by solving other people's problems. Customers and partners are eternally interested in their own problems, and the "busy" excuse does not solve any of them.

"Busy" phrases often serve as socially acceptable code for, "I am too important to give you my undivided attention", or, "I simply have not come through for you as promised", or, "I really cannot deliver for you." They also allow for avoidance of confrontation, which does not win respect, but is a luxury we often allow each other nonetheless.

However, a busy person who delivers and does not complain breaks the mold and stands out above all others. Imagine times you have been in the checkout line at the grocery store. You may have noticed one clerk moving people through faster and more efficiently than others. Then, you saw other customers leave the line they were in, move over to that line and still get out quickly.

We all want to do business with people like that. If you are that way, you need not worry about what the future holds for you.

FedEx guarantees overnight delivery for you, regardless of how "busy" they are. The market consistently rewards their operational excellence, efficiency and reliability with billions of dollars in profits for doing so.

To break the mold and rise above your competition, just deliver without complaint or excuse. If you do, you will be valued and in demand. And rare. Here is how:

> 1. *Define your priorities and make them clear.* Leave no question regarding your role, decisions you will make, or actions you will take, in the context of your other commitments. Commit that decision or action to a time and date, and avoid leaving it ambiguous if at all possible. Hold yourself to it and have the courage to invite accountability for it.

> 2. *Be a "NOW" person!* Nobody is perfect. But a service-oriented attitude combined with efficiency is refreshing and uncommon. I have a contract partner who is genuinely very busy, but it never shows in the way he handles my requests. He is a NOW person. If it can be done now, do it now.

> 3. *Engage yourself in meaningful activities.*

People who love what they do almost never use the "busy" excuse. So, do what you love and get good at it. If you are not doing what you love, make a change.

4. *Quit speaking in code and just be honest.* Don't string people along using the "busy" excuse. Show respect for the time and intelligence of others. If something is not a priority for you, just say so. If you can't get it done, just say so. Suggest another resource or way to proceed.

Breaking the Mold, Part 2

Voicemail

"I'm either on the phone, in a meeting, or away from my desk…"

No kidding.

I don't care, and neither does anyone else. I called to talk to you.

However, this voicemail is the standard, the mold. And if you work for a large organization or corporation, even if you are responsible for getting sales, you may not feel that you have room for creativity, so you fall back on the standard. You likely have to adhere to a corporate "dress code" in attitude and all forms of communication.

Even worse is a company with two message systems. The first is a computer that answers my call and tells me to listen carefully, because "our menu options have changed." Then, I can select from the following nine options "for my convenience and to serve me better." Then, I get dumped into your voicemail to hear about your meetings, your lunch hour, or how you are out of the office.

Or worse still, a live person answers the phone and dumps me into your voicemail without bothering to tell me that you are not there.

You get it by now. This annoys all of us, but we do it to each other anyway.

This presents an opportunity for you to break the mold, because your competitors are probably doing this too. You can underwhelm or irritate people who call you OR you can convert them into quality leads. And leads are not easy or cheap to obtain, so why not use your voicemail to generate them?

If you do not have to live under a rigid communication "dress code" as I described above, consider bringing your voicemail back to life. Here are some ideas.

1. A customer testimonial. Imagine one of your best customers saying something like, "Hello, I am John Smith from XYZ Construction. Jane is taking care of my account like she has for the last five years, and does a great job. She can take care of

16

yours too, so leave a message and she will be happy to help you."

2.   Your child. "Hello, this is Olivia. My dad, James is out working hard to earn my college tuition. You can help by leaving a big order at the tone."

3.   A thoughtful quote. There are available everywhere online. Try to change it daily.

4.   A fact about your product or service. Offer a hint or a tip on how your caller can use it or profit from it.

5.   Something funny, but use discretion. "Joe's voicemail is broken. This is his refrigerator. Please speak very slowly, and I'll stick your message to him on myself with one of these magnets."

6.   Take the opportunity to highlight your difference. If you are brave enough, you can say something like this: "Thank you for calling Triumph Business Communications. If your public relations needs are limited to someone who looks good in a miniskirt to represent you at your next nightclub event or tradeshow, please look elsewhere. We wish you the best of luck in your endeavors. However, if you need to tell the story of the great value that you provide, we can help you. We'll discuss it further when we call you back."

Some more rules:
1. Script it, rehearse it, and then record it.
2. Keep it as brief as possible.
3. Change it regularly.

4. Listen to the recorded comments carefully for reactions. The reactions of your customers will let you know whether or not your message was effective.

Your voicemail provides you with yet another opportunity to break the mold.

Reference: Gitomer, Jeffrey. "Fix your voice message now!" www.gitomer.com

Breaking the Mold, Part 3

Credentials

"REQUIRED: Master's degree and at least five years' experience…"

Do requirements like this always result in the best people for the job? Do they always bring you the best salespeople, the best leaders, the most skilled problem-solvers, or the highest quality service?

Perhaps from a Human Resources perspective, yes. They use diplomas and years of experience as crude job applicant screening tools. Hiring and HR managers pick through resumes and screen out candidates according to real or perceived flaws, or have software that filters the resumes. The software lacks the imagination to think of any other possibilities, so it falls back on credentials, and then the managers fall back on the software.

But most of the time, customers and co-workers don't care about your credentials. In most fields, credentials matter much, much less that the *ability to deliver*. Of even greater importance than that is the *willingness to deliver*.

We have all known professionals with years of experience who lacked energy and responsiveness, and many with stellar academic credentials who could not be relied upon or trusted any further than you could spit. Credentials alone never provide anything close to the full story of someone's reliability, ethics, or strength.

When I was a Marine Corps public affairs officer, I had a senior enlisted Marine public affairs specialist who I worked with on a daily basis. Master Sergeant (MSgt) **Tim Shearer** had nearly two decades of service as a combat correspondent that included several sea deployments, combat, and drill instructor duty but no college degree. He handled everyone, including me, with blunt, straightforward, and often colorful language. Sometimes, he rubbed people the wrong way, but nobody faulted his intentions and people of all ranks found him smart and sought his advice. I could always count on his presence in a pinch, the accuracy of his assessments, his journalistic skills, and the quality of the decisions we made together. His background did not fit the norm for public relations agencies, but he was among the most effective practitioners I have known. I learned much from him, and we remain friends today.

I was once invited to a university to participate in a "job fair" experience for students who were getting ready to graduate with Bachelor's degrees from the university's department of mass communications. I was asked to conduct mock job interviews with the students in order to help them to hone their interviewing skills.

I interviewed eight of them that day. They seemed eager but unseasoned and one-dimensional. I asked one girl why she chose to study mass communications, and her answer was, "…um, it was easier and I didn't want to take any hard math or science."

Impressed? Me neither.

Yet, for many public relations firms and employers of other industries, that degree is a non-negotiable requirement. That means that the girl in the example above will be hired and Tim would not be considered. She could be handling your account. At least she has a proven ability to spend four years following a syllabus and sitting in an auditorium.

By the way, the late Peter Jennings of ABC News rose to the top of broadcast journalism without a diploma. Brian Williams, the NBC news anchor and managing editor crushed the ratings against the famous University of Virginia graduate Katie Couric at CBS. Williams never earned a degree either. Abraham Lincoln was a self-taught lawyer. No degree.

Don't get me wrong. I went to school. There is nothing wrong with an education. It does expand one's knowledge and ability to think, and in the case of fields like sciences, business, engineering, medicine, it adds critical skills. Education imparts problem-solving ability, and a diploma shows commitment and some measure of determination. In some fields, academic credentials are important and rightly so. However, they do not tell the whole story, and probably not even the most important part of the story.

There are many ways to learn. Wisdom and grace can appear where you don't expect it, just as competence does. Conversely, competence, wisdom and grace sometimes fail to show where it normally is expected. Breaking the mold means striking out, challenging the norm, and daring the system.

How can you best choose associates, partners or employees? Break the mold. Loosen up about the diplomas and years of experience. Look a little deeper.

1. Take the time to build rapport. Everybody has a story, and people like telling theirs. Give them a chance to do that. It is an investment of time, but it is better than a bad hire. Feel them out with honest conversation and see if there is enough common reality and life experience between you.
2. Rely on the recommendations of trusted associates, and I do emphasize "trusted." If you know them to have everyone's best interest at heart, it saves you hours of screening and a lot of pain later. Skills and procedures can be taught, but someone with ethics that are wholly inconsistent with your own or those of your organization can cause lasting damage.
3. Present them with a problem and see how they respond. Give them a minor task and see how they work. Do you like the approach? The enthusiasm? The thought process?
4. Watch how they handle other people. Watch how

they talk about other people. It will provide accurate insight as to how they will handle people and talk about them, including you.
5. Get examples of their past work and ask them for the stories behind it.

Do this, and you just might find yourself surrounded by people who break the mold with you.

Chapter 3 Getting Things Done Through People Who Do Not Care

Think of the last time you achieved something significant.

How did you do it? Do you remember the force you put behind it?

At the risk of evoking a memory of a ubiquitous and overexposed motivational poster and a cliche, the force you put behind it was made possible by passion. Passion is the force behind every uncommon achievement.

Passion is transferrable and contagious. It makes you creative, which makes you find ways to do things. It makes you persistent, and only the persistent qualify for the prize. Persistence wins others over.

If your dream is significant, you cannot get it done by yourself. Between the present and the future you want is a collection of people. They will not get involved in your dreams without rewards. Those relationships are going to require constant exchange. You give up one thing to get another.

In fact, your entire life has been one of continuous exchange. You are giving up time to read this right now. You have given something for whatever you have, and others have too.

Success means knowing what to give up in exchange for what you want. Let us assume you are an entrepreneur. You may have exchanged a steady job, maybe a corporate job for the unknown. You decided that you would rather "pursue your passion instead of a pension." You gave up everything about corporate life that you did not like, but you also gave up the corporate paycheck and benefits.

Really, that is a lot of security to exchange. The future you want will require a lot of experiences with other people. Some will sponsor you in some way. Some will assist you and invest in you.

Others will hate your dream; they will despise it for whatever reason. They will most likely be subtle about this, finding ways to undermine it and suppress it behind the scenes. Or they will just discourage you. You will be tempted to internalize their words of unbelief. Don't. Better yet, *disconnect from them and remove them from your life*.

The difference between people who succeed and people who fail is those who they have chosen to believe.

So, how do you get things done through people who don't care?

We are not talking about adversaries. We are talking about people who are passive, who don't care, and who don't want to cooperate.

The answer is that your passion must be greater than their apathy. Proceed with authority and intent.

Start asking questions. The art of influencing people includes asking the right questions and giving them an opportunity to come up with answers that are consistent with yours. The questions you ask determine what you hear, what you see, and what you discover.

People who don't want to cooperate will blow you off. You may hear answers along these lines:
"Send me a proposal and I'll look at it".
"This does not fit our standard."
"This is not consistent with the direction we are moving in."
"This is not what we normally do."

By the way, it is easier to be courageous about "standards" and "direction" behind the relative safety of a long distance phone call, e-mail or gatekeeper. It is easier to blow you off behind the relative safety of a phone call, voicemail, e-mail, or gatekeeper. *Remove that relative safety whenever possible with a face to face encounter.*

Don't be afraid to do this. If you can't, then don't be afraid to work around them. Sure, there is a risk of offending or irritating them. But the possible reward is much greater.

Assess the risk/reward equation carefully. If you must make mistakes, do so more often on the side of pursuing the reward.

They will break your focus with small talk, with drinks, with lunch. Stick with the questions. Don't let them veer off the questions.

"The dark side puts up walls and has you believe that they are made of steel. In reality, they are made with paper mache". –Colin Powell

Success is not guaranteed, but you can penetrate someone's wall of apathy and get further and faster with uncommon passion and uncommon moxie.

Be unstoppable. You had it right when you were a baby, before the world taught you that persistence is pesky. Learn from a baby. A baby does not stop crying until her need is met.

Is there a step by step process? Again, success is not guaranteed, but you can greatly increase your probability of success. *Here are five ways to achieve through people who don't care:*

1. *Identify them*. Don't deceive yourself about who they are. You can identify them by their reactions to your requests. A good reaction will sound like this, "We don't know how, but are willing to figure it out. What do we need to do?" On the other hand, apathy sounds like this, "Our process prevents us." *If you get a response like that, ask them to put that in writing. That forces them to document their own inability*. There are people who don't care if you ever get what you want. Be honest with yourself about who they are. Move them from your life if you must.

2. *Give them an opportunity to learn and to develop passion*. In the case of someone who works with you or for you, give them an opportunity to be mentored. No one ever cared about them, so they don't care about others. It is all that was ever modeled for them. Bureaucracies and middle management of large organizations everywhere are packed with people who are *masters at adaptation but not achievement*. Teach them how to respond to you.

3. *Discern their level of competence*. Maybe they can't actually perform. Maybe they don't know how. Something may be easy for you, but that does not mean it is easy for others. Maybe they have never been trained. If not, accept that. Accept their limitations. It is hard to get someone to rise above the limitations they

think they have. Sometimes, it takes an incremental approach.

4. *Search for the replacement*. You do not have to keep everyone in your life. Some people are seasonal. Identify them. If someone keeps doing it wrong, look for someone who will do it right.

5. *Recognize and reward those who do care*. Don't get so busy with the squeaky wheel that you forget those who do care. There are some who want to do everything they can to be a part of your dream. You did not get here alone. There are people who love you but can't say it. There are people in your life who care about your goal and never told you. There are people who support you always but don't tell you. That's right! There are people who believe in you, fight for you, and lay awake at night thinking of ways to help you. There are people in the world who consider you valuable. *Don't forget them!* Don't take them for granted. Don't take your eyes off of them and onto those who don't care. Reward them with words, time, access, notes or gifts. There are people working for you that you don't know about, doing things that you do not see. Take a look at those who have brought you to where you are. Thank them. Reward those who have invested in your life.

Reference: Dr. Murdock, Mike, "We All Possess An Inner Invisible Thrust To Achieve". www.thewisdomcenter.tv/

Chapter 4 Boot Camp

It has been stated that the U.S. Marine Corps has two missions: making Marines and winning battles. To make Marines, they must first be recruited and then trained at boot camp, or recruit training. Recruit training is commonly known as boot camp, and those terms are used interchangeably.

Recruits who enlist west of the Mississippi River are sent to boot camp at Marine Corps Recruit Depot San Diego, CA. Recruiting responsibility for that part of the U.S. is headquartered at San Diego as well, and so that is the Western Recruiting Region.

Recruits who enlist east of the Mississippi River come to Parris Island, SC, and the Eastern Recruiting Region is headquartered there. So, the commanding general (CG) in San Diego is responsible for meeting the recruiting mission (quota) and for training the recruits for the entire Western U.S.

The CG at Parris Island has the same responsibility in the Eastern U.S.: recruiting, training, and graduating them. Additionally, all female Marine recruits train at Parris Island.

"Does boot camp prepare you for war? Is there applicability to business or life?"

Marine Corps boot camp is extremely demanding, both physically and mentally. I enlisted in the Marine Corps reserve when I was 17 and went to boot camp at Parris Island within days of graduating high school. I stayed in the reserve throughout college and lost a year of college when my reserve unit was activated. We went on a combat deployment to the Middle East and fought in the first Gulf War in 1990-1991. I returned from Saudi Arabia and Kuwait feeling like a changed and much older man at 21.

I will not recount that here in any great depth. I can tell you that it was harsh, dirty, ugly, exhilarating at times, and deadly serious. I can also tell you that boot camp prepares you for that kind of stress.

It is easier to appreciate the comforts of home. Life seemed easier in many ways after coming home from something like that, if you are fortunate enough to come home in one piece, as I was. I realize that this will sound melodramatic, but tonight, if I have a clean place to sleep, a roof over my head, and nobody trying to kill me, it is good. Combat veterans understand that.

Crisis is in the eye of the beholder...it is relative. People can be trained, prepared, and made stronger in preparation for a fight. Just as exercise can fatigue muscles before they grow stronger, the soul is transformed and matured as a result of extreme trial. Military service in a combat zone will alter one's perspective on stress and what a crisis really is. Later in life, if there is no mortal danger, it does not feel like a crisis. Having a thicker hide does not mean failing to give problems their due attention, but the emotional perspective on problems is more measured.

You know people who are just not strong and are ruled by their emotions. To them, crisis is everywhere. I thought about this while working in a bank many years later and watching someone cry hysterically because a customer was mean to her.

There is greatness to be found in ordinary people in times of extraordinary stress. The fight exposes greatness and somehow develops it as well. I see greatness in people who run toward danger instead of away from it.

I made friends during that war that I will always have-- guys who would do anything to make sure that I came home alive and in one piece and I would do the same for them. We became close, passing the time with hours of conversation and a lot of humor, laughing uproariously over things that were salty, crude, and often morbid. The guys in my platoon taught me that it is okay, even healthy, to laugh in the face of danger.

The Foxhole Test

I saw what happens when people put the safety and well-being of others before their own. It creates deep trust. I have friends who are veterans, and we occasionally talk about good and evil and various people in our lives. We talk about the *"foxhole test."*

Picture yourself in a foxhole, or fighting hole with someone...a defensive position. You are either under attack or expecting an attack. Will they have your back or flee for their own safety, leaving you by yourself? Can you count on someone who is there with you? *How will that person handle extreme adversity?*

This is a high standard. It is applicable in business, in relationships, and in life. Here are the guidelines:

1. **Commitment**. Is someone on board with your goals and committed to your achievement of them? What are they willing to do to help you get there? Are they strong and unchanging in their support, or fickle, changing with moods? Your cause may change and they may not be on board with that, but if you know exactly where you stand with a person that is what you want.
2. **Decisiveness**. This refers to speed and quality of decision making. A strong leader will not leave you hanging.
3. **Transparency**. Everybody must deliver bad news sometimes. How is that task handled? When you follow through with him, does he respond? Or does he hide behind voicemail, e-mail or an assistant? Does she duck an issue and

hope you will just "get it" and figure it out on your own because she does not want confrontation? It takes no courage to slow-walk something to death. A strong leader knows how to provide clear but gracious finality.

4. **Fairness**. Someone who is consistently fair in an unfair world is someone worth having in your life. This is someone who does not apply different standards to themselves as they do for you. Such people account for your interests as well as their own.

5. **Communication about others and with you**. How a person talks about others behind their back is an indicator of how they talk about you behind your back. Do you feel the presence of hostility that you cannot identify? Or is there a clean space between you that is free of guile, mystery, or unresolved issues?

We all fall short of each other's hopes and expectations from time to time. Everybody has moments of weakness, but the strong don't run from their moments of weakness. They don't justify them, blame others for them, or dodge responsibility for them. They own up to them, learn from them, and look for ways to profit and improve from them.

You have people in your life that fall too short too often. Be honest with yourself about whom they are and keep a healthy distance. Be honest with yourself and apply it to yourself, too.

Use the foxhole test to protect yourself in business, relationships, and life.

You have probably seen the World War II image of Marines (and one Navy corpsman) planting the American flag on top of Mount Suribachi. The Marine Corps Memorial in Washington, D.C. is a statue of it. You have seen it on magazine covers and postage stamps; it is an iconic symbol of American victory. That was near the conclusion of an extremely bloody battle against entrenched Japanese forces on the island of Iwo Jima in the Pacific in March, 1945. Marines fought a literal uphill battle and planted the flag to show that the island was secure and in American hands.

The guys that fought their way up the mountain did not do that for democracy. They did not do it for America, or the flag, or the Constitution. Such things are distant abstractions while in a fight. They fought their way up that mountain for each other. They fought to protect the guys on the left and right, and the guys on the left and right fought to protect them as they advanced.

Units are made strong collectively by making the warriors within them as individually strong as possible. Warriors, whether from America or any other civilization or time in history, have trained and fought as units. Military success will not happen any other way.

Back to Boot Camp

Now, let's go back to Parris Island. Boot camp is the place to burn off selfishness, self-centeredness, self-indulgence, and other undesirable human qualities that start with "self."

At boot camp, young people are trained hard together. Hardship is shared. Stress is shared. Deprivation is shared. It is meant to create bonds between Marines that are so strong that they indeed fight as unstoppable units. Everything that happens there has a purpose and a reason. The process has another benefit. Boot camp produces better people. Marines return back to society as better citizens.

Boot camp is three phases. Phase one is week one through four. During that time, recruits who arrived as civilians are immersed into Marine Corps culture. The night they arrive, they give up their civilian clothes and are issued uniforms and gear. Male recruits have their heads shaved bald. They receive medical and dental screenings and exams. They undergo strenuous physical training and martial arts training, along with water survival. They also receive classes on first aid, Marine Corps history, and other subjects. Everywhere they go and for everything they do, they are subject to drill instructors (DIs) yelling, insulting, barking orders, demanding total obedience, and making them move NOW!

At five AM, the entire platoon wakes up to incandescent overhead lights and the sounds of screaming DIs. The DIs give the platoon exactly one minute to be completely dressed: shirts, blouses, trousers, boots laced up and tied. The DIs count down one minute amid frantic activity and it never fails. At the end of the one minute the DI says, "Zero!" That means freeze. Looking around the room, a handful may actually be fully dressed. The rest of the recruits stand there in various phases of partial dress, some with trousers halfway up, one boot may be on and completely laced while the other is not. Some have blouses or shirts on inside out if they are on at all.

The platoon did not perform this simple task fast enough. The DIs order them to strip and do it again and again until the entire platoon is dressed in under a minute. Then, they make racks (beds). Again, they have a minute to accomplish this perfectly, with the white sheet folded over the green wool blanket, exactly 12 inches from the head of the mattress. The pillow must be folded properly within the pillowcase and centered at the head of the mattress. The sheets and blanket must be tucked in tight, not unlike a hospital bed.

A few will do it. The rest? Not fast enough or good enough. The DIs order the platoon to strip their racks and do it again RIGHT NOW! And again and again, until something noticeable happens.

The ones who accomplish it quickly start to help the ones who don't. In fact, every task the platoon does, they begin to pull each other through. It could be cleaning rifles, physical training, cleaning buildings, whatever.

Phase two is week five through nine. This is when the recruits receive marksmanship training. Marksmanship is two weeks. During the second week, they fire the M-16 rifles and qualify. Later they undergo combat survival training where they learn combat marksmanship, land navigation, and maneuvering under enemy fire. They also learn how to rappel and to use a gas mask.

Phase three is week nine through twelve. During this time, they are tested via "practical application." This means that they are tested on various tasks such as first aid by physically performing them for grade, as opposed to written tests. They go to the Confidence Course (I personally loved it), which is a series of 11 large obstacles that includes the Skyscraper (it resembles a massive ladder in which the recruits climb up one side and down the other), the Slide for Life (a little like a zip line, but negotiated with hands and feet) and others that incorporate gymnastic-like skills to negotiate.

They take a final physical fitness test (PFT) and undergo a final close-order drill evaluation and competition. Close-order drill is essential to teach recruits to perform as a unit. They march from place to place in formation. The DI calls a cadence (rhythmic commands in a song form that keeps a formation in step and in unison), "left, right, left right, march." When the DI says, "left", every recruit steps with the left foot. This is done with precision, which grows with each day. Drill incorporates rifle carriage. For example, "left shoulder arms" is a command to lean the rifle against your shoulder at a 45 degree angle while marching.

Several hours each week are devoted to close order drill. It teaches precision, teamwork, and discipline.

The Crucible is the graduation exercise and is the week before graduation. It is 54 hours and includes everything the recruits learned in boot camp. It incorporates obstacles that can only be negotiated through teamwork. It also features day and night marches, night infiltration courses, leadership tests,

Core values training, combat simulations, and all of it is done with two and a half meals and four hours of sleep. At the conclusion of the Crucible, the recruits attend a ceremony where they are awarded an Eagle, Globe and Anchor emblem, the symbol of the Marine Corps. They are addressed as "Marine" for the first time.

The recruits undergo final inspections and then graduate with a parade and a ceremony. Then, they are allowed to go home for ten days before infantry training.

I had done some recruiting and contracted boys who were slovenly, overweight, and heading absolutely nowhere in life. However, they were willing to radically change direction. Completion of boot camp represented a major accomplishment for kids like that, and the start of a transformed life.

Graduation is emotional for recruits and their families. I have seen parents barely able to recognize their sons. Long hair, obesity, slouching, poor manners, and lack of direction have been replaced by clean high and tight haircuts, physically fit bodies, military posture, respect and confidence. Every graduation features scenes of mothers and fathers with tears of happiness in their eyes, profusely thanking drill instructors.

So, that is a sanitized rundown of the training schedule but it does not capture the complete experience.

"Everything has a purpose."

The training schedule does not tell the story of the stress. It is mentally and emotionally demanding because the drill instructors create that environment. They demand obedience through harsh leadership, screaming, yelling, and creating constant urgency and artificial stress. That is done for several reasons, and all of them benefit the recruits.

Artificial adversity teaches people to unite and come together, so that in times of real adversity, they know how to rely and to be reliable.

Artificial stress prepares you for real stress. If you learn to perform while someone is screaming at you in order to break your focus, you will learn coolness under fire.

If you are forced to stretch beyond your personal comfort zone to achieve something that you never could before, you will gain courage and confidence.

If someone presses your emotional hot buttons enough, they may become less effective as hot buttons.

If you are forced to get up early whether or not you "feel like it," then your day will be more productive than if left to your own devices.

If you are forced to perform whether or not you are "in the mood" to do it, your life takes on added vitality.

This is how new habits and mindsets are formed, and they create a foundation for disciplined living. If used properly, that discipline translates to accomplishment that might not have happened otherwise.

Boot camp is disorienting and shocking for a reason. "No, son! Salute with your RIGHT hand!" The kid is scared and intimidated and presents an awkward attempt at a salute with his left hand. He is focused only on the stress, so much so that he cannot follow simple instructions. "What is wrong with you? What was your recruiter thinking when he sent you here? WHAT PLANET ARE YOU FROM? Show me your right hand and salute!"

Today's war heroes will tell you that at one time they were just scared kids arriving at boot camp.

Each platoon of recruits is normally assigned at least two DIs plus a senior drill instructor (SDI). The SDI is the mentor. The SDI can be harsh too, but it is a leadership role for the other DIs and the recruits.

There are three platoons in a series. A series commander is responsible for the three platoons of recruits and DIs, and oversees them. The series commander teaches classes to the recruits, supervises physical training, enforces the Standard Operating Procedure, and as a commissioned officer involved in the training of recruits, serves as an officer role model. He is present throughout the entire cycle.

The series commander is assisted by a series gunnery sergeant, also known as a series chief drill instructor. The series gunnery sergeant leads physical training for the series and supervises close order drill.

If a recruit fails to perform, lapses in discipline, or makes a mistake, the recruit may be subject to Incentive Physical Training (IPT). IPT is a series of exercises: pushups, mountain climbers, leg lifts, side straddle hops, running in place. IPT can be administered in the barracks (building where the recruits live), in a shaded area near a parade deck, or in a partitioned area filled with sand, known as "the pit."

"Oh? You don't want to move fast? Get in the pit NOW!"
"Aye, sir!"
"More VOLUME! Get in the pit NOW!"
"AYE, SIR!"
"PUSHUPS NOW! Push push push push push! Up down up down up down up down! Faster now!"
"AYE SIR!"
"LOUDER, RECRUIT! FASTER, RECRUIT! Do you hear me? I want to see speed! Urgency! Now run in place! Faster! Knees higher! Higher!"

After five minutes, the recruit emerges from the impromptu "workout" sweaty and dirty. "You may not be smart, but you will be strong!"

You get the picture. The senior drill instructor can put the entire platoon in the pit if they are performing poorly. They will put the entire platoon in the pit if only a handful of recruits are inattentive or performing poorly. That turns the attention of the platoon on the underperformers.

Did most of the platoon fail inspection? Put them in the pit. Are they performing close order drill sluggishly? Put them in the pit and wake them up.

The SDI is also the one who talks to them at night and answers their questions. He helps them with problems. He allows them an occasional laugh. He is their mentor.

Female recruit training is set up exactly the same, but they are trained apart from the male recruits. The male and female recruits are kept strictly isolated and apart from each other.

"Sir, do I really have to go there?"

Sometimes, life forces you in the right direction whether you want it to or not.

I stayed in the Marine Corps reserve and graduated from Florida State University. By now, I was a sergeant and I performed some recruiting duty in Tampa. Then, I went to Officer Candidate School (OCS) in Quantico, VA and was commissioned a second lieutenant.

OCS is very demanding and physical. It is like boot camp, but it is for officers and it is a screening process. You graduate lean and in fighting physical condition.

OCS resembles boot camp. It is close enough that I could say that I had been through boot camp twice and really did not care to return to that sort of environment.

However, I wanted to be a public affairs officer and was told that was possible. However, the need for that was at Parris Island. And before I could practice public affairs, I was needed on the drill field because there was a shortage of series commanders.

I agreed, with some attitude I might add. Before, I would have been happy to never see another man in a "Smokey Bear" hat. A guy can only take so much boot camp. Now, I would have to lead it.

I went to the two-week series commander's course at Drill Instructor School and was assigned to one of the recruit training battalions. I arrived a few days before our recruits arrived. For officers, command time is necessary for advancement and this was my first opportunity at command.

Yes, it helped that I had been enlisted and had combat experience, but I still had a lot to learn. I met the DIs and SDIs assigned to my series that I would work with, and my series gunnery sergeant.

I always relied on him, but especially for the first few weeks after assuming command. He knew his way around and told me that if I listened to him, we would all stay out of trouble. He would tell me, "Sir, here is where you need to be tomorrow morning and here is what we are going to do."

Before too long, I found that I was becoming excited to come to work. Every one of my DIs was simply awesome. Including nights where they were required to sleep on duty in the recruit barracks, they put in 120 hour work weeks. I never saw any of them tired; the energy was always "on." I would see one them berate a recruit in a savage way, leaving the recruit thinking that the DI was absolutely psychotic. But DIs are the kind of guys that will do that, then instantly turn it off in private, telling me with a calm voice and a smile behind closed doors that, "Sir, that's a good kid." Yes, there are theatrics involved.

We would move the recruits through the three month training cycle, graduate them, and start a week later with a new series of recruits. Then, I was experienced and became very comfortable with command. In fact, I grew to love it.

"Everybody has a story."

These kids enlisted for a variety of reasons: adventure, world travel, job training, college benefits, guts and glory, whatever. But all of them chose the Marine Corps instead of the other services and since I had done it myself and had some time recruiting, I had a good handle on why. They wanted the toughest boot camp. They were action oriented or wanted to be. They wanted the challenge; they wanted to better themselves.

These kids came to Parris Island to find their manhood.

Under the Standard Operating Procedure (SOP), I was required to interview each recruit under my command and submit a short report on each. A series had a maximum of 264 recruits, and sometimes I had that many kids under my command, so the interviews could be a time consuming task, spaced out over the three months. The questions were always the same. They were primarily a check against abuse or hazing, and to ensure that their basic needs were met.

"At any time while at Parris Island, have you been punched, kicked, or slapped? Have you been getting three meals daily? Have you been afforded an opportunity to attend religious services? Have you ever been denied medical attention? Have you been able to send and receive mail? Have you ever been denied water? Is your senior drill instructor taking care of you? Is there anything going on that you need to tell me about?"

The recruits would answer those questions "yes" or "no." I also asked, "Why did you decide to join the Marine Corps?"

I always listened closely. I heard stories of wanting to grow up, stories of boredom with college, stories of poor home environments. I heard stories of escaping the inner city, stories of leaving rural areas, stories of rich parents, and stories of immigrant parents. I heard stories of abuse, gang life, of poverty, and a lot of motivation for a better life.

To outsiders, these kids look the same and seem interchangeable. After all, they are all dressed in the same uniforms, with the exact same haircuts.

But every one of them has a story. Just like you.

Chapter 5 Managing a High Volume of Media Interest

I was a series commander for nearly a year. Then, I went to the public affairs office. I had already completed the public affairs officer course which included journalism and most of the necessary skills of public relations.

My role there was to be the media officer. There was constant media interest at Parris Island, and after a year as a series commander, I knew the place well. I knew the culture and many of the DIs.

So, I was constantly escorting media, arranging interviews for them, and often going on the record myself, answering reporters' questions about recruiting and recruit training. I monitored the stories they published, I prepared DIs, recruits, colonels, generals or whomever for interviews. I wrote talking points and press releases.

I began to notice that a few reporters, not understanding or respecting what we were doing, would make some requests that seemed bothersome.

I was asked to tell a DI to yell at a kid just for some footage.

I saw cameramen get too close to recruits firing with live ammunition on the rifle range. The last thing we need is for a kid shooting for the first time to have that sort of distraction.

Reporters wanted footage of themselves on an obstacle course. After seeing a couple of stories like that, they looked the same. One was especially painful. It was one take after another of a female reporter with no athletic ability giggling and screaming while falling off an obstacle into the arms of a Marine waiting to catch her.

Reporters and cameramen asked to accompany recruits into the barracks at night (where they are sometimes undressed) and interview them during their one hour of free time.

We came up with three guidelines:

1. *Never stage events for reporters*. If it happens in front of them, that is fine. But if the event (like the DI berating a recruit) is staged just for them, it will not look authentic because it is not authentic.
2. *Never compromise safety or interfere with training or operations*. In the case of the

cameraman who entered the firing line and got too close, I grabbed him, loaded his equipment into the van, and escorted him off the base.

3. *Never violate propriety*. No footage of recruits undressed and no violations of privacy.

You may find them applicable for your organization as well.

I worked with a lot of media. They included CNN, ABC News, major city newspapers, and television, and some media from places like Japan, Uruguay and Argentina.

In 2000, Dreamworks Studios became interested in producing a miniseries about Marines which would start at boot camp. It was called *Semper Fi* and they wanted to film it as a movie on location at Parris Island. The major part of the casting had been done. **Keith David** would star as the senior drill instructor, and some of the recruits included **Michael Pena**, **Steve Burton**, and **Bianca Kajlich**. We provided support for that, including technical advice. They held a casting call for some of the other parts, such as extras to play the part of other recruits. They also needed a male and female series commander. I auditioned and won the part and played the series commander in the movie.

There had been other movies about Parris Island, such as *The D.I.* (1957) and *Full Metal Jacket* (1987).

After several months as the media officer, Parris Island had another shortage of series commanders, so I went back to the drill field and trained recruits. Then, there was an issue of SOP violations at another battalion that resulted in some DIs and officers relieved of duty. So, I transferred to that battalion which was shorthanded, and a cautious, "by the book" sort of atmosphere prevailed there.

It was a leadership challenge, but I loved the drill field. It was very demanding but it felt like somewhat of a ministry. By now, I was a captain and I felt somewhat torn because I was asked if I was interested in commanding a company, which is two series. I liked being close to the action, and commanding a company would take me away from it.

I had trained over a thousand young men by now and overseen about three dozen drill instructors. We protected the DIs and recruits; not one allegation of mistreatment. In the prior two years, the Drill Instructor of the Year of each year was one of mine personally. I had written recommendation letters for exceptional recruits, which helped those young men to win ROTC (Reserve Officers Training Corps) scholarships, appointments at the U.S. Naval Academy, and acceptance to commissioning programs.

One day, MSgt Tim Shearer at the public affairs office sent me this e-mail: "Sir, the major's office was painted." I responded with words to the effect of, "So why are you telling me this?" He replied, "Because the major's office will be your new office."

The public affairs director left to take another assignment on short notice, so I was now responsible for it. The responsibilities included the base newspaper, the visitor's center, the media, marketing for recruiting for half the country and I was now on the general's staff. But that meant that I was finished on the drill field and it was honestly a sad day.

To do this job, I had a public affairs chief who was an experienced enlisted combat correspondent. I had a media officer. I had combat correspondents: Marines who were trained as photojournalists who wrote stories for the base newspaper. I had another who was a webmaster and another who was skilled at editing and layout for the base newspaper. I had some sharp looking Marines who manned the Visitors Center, helping thousands of family members who showed up each week for graduation and I had a civilian employee.

Chapter 6 "Late Night" Cadence

Shortly after taking this job, I received a call from a producer from *The Late Show with David Letterman*. They wanted us to send them a drill instructor. I asked why, and he said that they thought it would be funny and great television to have the DI run around and berate the band and yell at members of the audience.

We don't participate in caricatures of boot camp. My chief of staff and CG agreed and we said "no thanks."

A couple of months later, I received another call from them. This time, it was a different producer. He told me that **David Letterman** was patriotic and admired the Marine Corps. He explained that Letterman liked to run in New York's Central Park while playing and listening to a Marine Corps drill instructor sing cadence. Would we be able to locate this drill instructor and agree to let him be a guest on the show?

I asked what cadence it was. We found it, and it had been recorded in 1975, so it would be hard to find that man. He then asked if we could find someone similar. He had to be "soulful" and, he added somewhat sheepishly, black.

I said maybe, but under no circumstances would any DI participate in a skit or be asked to do anything that would embarrass him or us. The producer agreed and I asked him to send me an e-mail to confirm that agreement.

I got to work selling the idea to the chain of command, my chief of staff, general, and the Pentagon. I had brought up Letterman in previous staff meetings and mid-level officers who were part of the general's staff panned the idea.

I wasn't sure why, but a handful of these officers (majors, lieutenant colonels and colonels) seemed to oppose the idea of media attention at Parris Island at every turn. It almost seemed reflexive, born of risk aversion or personal conservatism. However, they sure liked appearing in the base newspaper.

Such is life practicing public affairs in a large organization like government or the military.

I worked around those officers and eventually gained support for the idea. I asked the Recruit Training

Regiment to help me find some suitable DIs. They sent me six DIs who showed up at my office. I got the producer on speaker phone and had each DI sing cadence for him in an "audition" of sorts. It was entertaining and they all sounded great.

The producer selected one and arranged to bring the DI to New York City. The DI was flown there, picked up in a limousine and checked into a first class hotel. They also got a local Marine Corps reserve unit to send Marines to appear in formation on Broadway in front of the Ed Sullivan Theater. The DI sang cadence and ran them in formation into the theater, which was packed with Marines in dress blues. David Letterman greeted them all warmly. It was indeed patriotic, respectful, and represented everybody well.

This took place during the first week of September 2001; a bit of a sad irony considering what happened in New York City the following week.

Keys to Triumph

1. We insisted on an absolute standard of respect.
2. When they adapted, we did too.

Chapter 7 Discovery Channel

We received another call earlier that summer from a documentary producer named **Chuck Braverman**. He wanted to document some recruits, from enlistment all the way through boot camp. That meant total access and a lot of work for us, since reporters and camera crews are escorted by someone from our office at all times while on the base.

My public affairs chief MSgt. Tim Shearer was on the phone with him and I heard his end of the conversation. A combat correspondent and former DI himself, Shearer lacked patience, as I did for anyone proposing to portray us in anything less than an accurate light. He had a good sense of how to tell the story of recruiting and boot camp. I heard him say dryly to the man on the phone, "We are here to support you because the public has a right to know what we are doing, but we are not here to support all of your creative and theatrical needs."

I had to leave the room because I was laughing too hard.

However, Braverman's proposal had merit. We would have the recruiters identify some kids and allow the producer to interview them at home before they arrived at Parris Island. They would be kids from New York City, Tennessee, and other places. Once the recruits arrived at Parris Island, we would supervise the story from there until they graduated.

The experience of the 13-week boot camp is transformative. It is normally a time of rapid personal growth and change for recruits. This training is designed to be a personal "makeover" in many ways. While the experience is generally the same for all, it is intensely personal.

Recruits enter Parris Island as young civilians and graduate as U.S. Marines. The title really is earned, and it is not earned until a recruit is smartly disciplined, physically fit, and well-trained. How this is done is something to behold. I once heard a drill instructor refer to it as human alchemy. There is constant media interest in the human side of it.

Reporters of all media and markets want to see, photograph, and film snarling, screaming drill instructors swarming around recruits while barking orders and berating them. They want footage of recruits low-crawling in slithering movement through dirt and mud. They air images of recruits climbing obstacles, shooting rifles, practicing infantry tactics, and executing close-order drill. By the way, they find female recruits doing all of these things to be especially compelling, so female recruit training is in high demand among media. And reporters always want to interview recruits and drill instructors on the record asking them just why they volunteer for it.

Every recruit is treated equally. Nobody gets special accommodations, food, privileges, treatment or consideration of any kind. Race, culture, religion, socioeconomic status, or who your parents are is of zero relevance. This treatment is one of the ways that the Marine Corps replaces civilian selfishness with a military ethic of putting others and unit before self. Parris Island does not graduate spoiled kids.

Certainly, all of this is in contrast to the society from which these young people came, volunteered to defend, and will one day return to. At Parris Island, that contrast and that transformation is an appropriate story. If media published stories that reflected that, I considered that to be accurate coverage and a success.

Braverman hoped to sell the documentary to the *Discovery Channel* and he told me of his track record. I knew that this documentary would be a major effort for everyone, but it was worth it. We agreed to support it, and obtained cooperation from the Recruiting Command as well.

Braverman was based in New York City. Some of these kids were from the New York City boroughs of Queens and Brooklyn. They came from working families. Two of them had parents who worked in Manhattan, in the area of the financial district.

The producer had interviewed these kids throughout the summer and documented a few days of each week that they were at boot camp. My media officer worked day and night to escort the film crew and facilitate their requests.

The film crew came down from New York for a couple of days each week interviewing their chosen recruits and DIs and gathering footage.

When we allow this kind of access, anything goes. If media is present and cameras are rolling, something may happen that you don't like. They own it and there is little that can be done to mitigate it.

Case in point: one frustrated recruit had recently had a profanity-laced meltdown while on a forced march, right in the presence of a CNN crew. "Fuck this shit, man! I want to go home!"

That is why you allow access to media that is willing to offer accommodations in return for receiving them. You need to make sure that you are working with someone with whom you have mutually acceptable ground rules. If something bad happens and you have it on the record, then let us mitigate it by providing you with a statement on the record, aired in its entirety, with no editing from you.

That is an example of a deal you can make with the media. Don't be so desperate for public attention that you fail to protect yourself!

On the morning of September 11, 2001, the film crew was headed to La Guardia Airport in New York for their weekly trip to spend with their recruits and us, but the events of that day delayed their travel for about three days.

Not that we would have been able to help them much that day anyway. Parris Island and other military facilities adopted a tight security posture and we had to decide what measures to disclose to the public and which ones not to. Did we need to cancel recruit graduations? It was uncharted territory, and Brigadier General (BGen) **Joseph J. McMenamin**, our CG had us in his conference room about an hour after the attacks. He said, "You all realize that everything is going to change completely after today." The military and indeed the entire government went into crisis mode and we spent the day answering frantic questions from media and parents of recruits. "Are you going to send recruits to Afghanistan as soon as they graduate? Is my son going to war?"

The answer was no of course. They had much more specialized training to accomplish after boot camp. Then, they would get assigned to units and nobody knew at that time what units might get deployed or even if they would.

When the Braverman crew did arrive, they interviewed the recruits on camera and got them talking about the possibility of going to war. In response to feelings of uncertainty, a couple of recruits began crying on camera, especially the one who had a parent who worked near the World Trade Center.

In early October, they graduated. Braverman produced a three hour documentary called, *Making Marines: Parris Island.* It was accurate, in-depth, and Chuck Braverman later told me that it won awards. It did indeed run on the *Discovery Channel* and did so often over the next couple of years. It can still be seen on some other networks such as the *Military Channel*.

The story was compelling, but the terrorist attacks added an especially compelling dimension to it.

Keys to Triumph

1. We knew a good opportunity when we heard it. *If you know your business well, you will develop a well-tuned antenna for opportunities to portray it accurately to the public.*
2. Braverman was cooperative and receptive to our suggestions on how to tell a story of "transformation." We just seemed to "Zen"; combining his notion of good documentary with our notion of accuracy.
3. *Well-chosen spokespersons, both demographically and otherwise*. The recruiters chose recruits wisely. I am certain that the documentary helped the recruiting effort then and still does all these years later.

Chapter 8 Crisis and Tragedy

As I said before, crisis is in the eye of the beholder and a recruit death is a tragic crisis. When something like that happens, it merits special attention and thorough investigation. In this case, a young man contracted meningitis and died two days before Christmas.

Recruits come to boot camp from various parts of the country and some of them may bring viruses with them, which can spread throughout the tight living conditions of the squad bay. One infected kid may touch a door handle and the rest of the platoon touches it too and becomes exposed. The DIs order thorough daily cleanings of the squad bay, but it can be a somewhat septic environment anyway.

One morning, a recruit on bed rest did not get up. The DIs called emergency medicine and he was eventually pronounced dead at Memorial Health University Medical Center in Savannah, GA, south of Parris Island.

Meningitis is inflammation of the protective membranes covering the brain and spinal cord. Those membranes are called the meninges. It is life threatening because the inflammation is so close to the brain and spinal cord. Common symptoms are headaches and stiffness of the neck.

In this case, the recruit had not shown signs of a stiff neck and had only complained of a headache. Early symptoms of it resemble the flu. To definitively diagnose it requires a blood culture. The recruit died quickly after reporting that he felt bad.

The issues were several. Was there something that could have been done to prevent it? In this case, he did not complain of a stiff neck. However, the recruit may have felt bad for a couple of days but did not report it until it was too late.

Meningitis occurs most often among young people, which certainly includes the recruit population. Did he have the contagious kind, and were other recruits at risk? A culture was done on him that indicated that this was not meningococcal bacterium which is contagious.

At any rate, he had a family and they were owed some answers, along with sincere condolences. The media began asking if this was associated with bioterrorism, which did not appear to be the case. They also began asking if there was a serious risk to other recruits. The story was in media around Savannah, Charleston, and the recruit's hometown.

In order to answer these concerns, I had an idea.

"Prophylaxis"

I decided to put together a public information campaign. I would put a Navy doctor or medical officer on camera, in uniform to explain briefly what meningitis is, what symptoms to look for, and how people could protect themselves.

To do this, I contacted a TV reporter that we had worked well with. I could count on her to not take an inflammatory tone toward a story. She was fair but accommodative. If an interview was not going well, I could always ask her to stop and allow the subject an opportunity to regroup.

I always had to coach people to *eliminate use of jargon during interviews*. Medical professionals often have bad jargon habits and must be coached not to use it with media.

We got the medical officer ready. He looked good— credible and convincing in his uniform. The reporter started the interview.

The medical officer said, "There is available prophylaxis that can prevent disease such as this."

I asked the reporter to stop the interview, which she did. Then I asked him what "prophylaxis" meant. He answered that it referred to preventative measures.

I told him that this story was being watched by people on their sofas at home who may not know what is meant by "prophylaxis" and maybe we should just say "preventative measures" instead. He said okay.

The reporter started over and the medical officer again began to talk about various prophylaxes.

Damn it. Please stop the interview. She did.

I turned to him and said, "Sir, I realize that you are talking about preventative measures and that is helpful to what we are trying to do here. The problem is that this particular word sounds very close to 'prophylactic' and everybody knows what that is. We can confuse people if we are not careful. Let's try to avoid making people think about condoms or sex today. Let's keep this simple and focused on meningitis. Do we need a few minutes to come up with some talking points?"

We started over. After two more takes, he got it right and pulled off a solid, informative interview.

Keys to Triumph

1. Don't accept a jargon-filled interview. It confuses people and is therefore useless. Stop it at every turn.
2. Whenever possible, work with reporters who know how to make a subject feel comfortable.

Hazing

There is a lot of attention on preventing any sort of hazing in boot camp. Drill instructors are normally Marines of the utmost professionalism and dedication. It is tremendously hard work.

Much is demanded of them and they demand much from the recruits. Occasionally, things get out of hand and SOP violations are alleged. They are always investigated thoroughly.

One day a young man in North Carolina showed up at his senator's office with quite a story to tell. He had just been discharged from the Marine Corps after about six months following a suicide attempt.

He had graduated from Parris Island about two or three months prior along with the rest of his platoon. What he told the senator resulted in a lengthy investigation.

He told a story of several weeks of mistreatment at the hands of drill instructors with the willful blindness of the senior drill instructor. He described the platoon awakened from sleep and pulled out of their racks at 3 AM and forced to run wind sprints up and down the rifle range. He described other acts of sadism, such as a DI forcing recruits to strip their racks of linen, take the linen into the shower room with the water running, soak the linen, and then make their racks with wet linen and sleep on it. He described DIs throwing Bibles and encouraging recruits to fight and haze each other. He also described pressure to keep all of it secret.

Apparently the bad blood continued after graduation and at the school of infantry where they went next. The social pressure proved to be too much for him, so he tried to hang himself but other Marines intervened.

He was discharged as a result. His mother wanted to alert the media, so she went to a TV station in Raleigh with one of those "investigator teams" of reporters. He was scheduled to be interviewed by them the next day. The recruiting station there called me quite concerned about it.

At the request of the senator's office, the Naval Criminal Investigative Service (NCIS) had started looking into it. They went to find these Marines who had been recruits in that platoon and took statements from them.

Meanwhile, we found the kid's military record. The suicide attempt resulted in a discharge for a "personality disorder." Ordinarily, military records are protected under the Privacy Act of 1974. They are not releasable to the public. However, a person can lose his rights under the Privacy Act if he voluntarily seeks media attention. That exception is there for a reason. Why should the government protect your privacy if you don't want it protected?

I held my nose and told the chief of staff of my plan, because I thought he would not like it. I told him that we could communicate privately with this young man. We could tell him that if he made allegations to the media about Parris Island that may yet prove unfounded (the investigation was not finished at the time, so we did not know if they were true), then he forfeited his rights under the Privacy Act. We could them release a statement saying that had a medical discharge but for reasons other than physical health. Reporters could read between the lines of such a statement and request his records, or ask him what that meant.

The chief of staff approved. I had the recruiting station find his recruiter, since this young man trusted him. The recruiting station told him that he risked the Marine Corps releasing the record of his suicide attempt if he went forward with the TV interview.

He cancelled the interview. There were no media stories about these allegations.

Keys to Triumph

1. This tactic felt personally distasteful, but it prevented a negative story.
2. There is always some tool at your disposal to use in your defense from bad press, but you have to look for it.

Chapter 9 Getting Things Done in Spite of the Risk Aversion of Someone Else

I have described how it is necessary to coordinate media efforts with other concerned parties. For the most part, I had carte blanche to approve media visits and itineraries. I always kept the chief of staff informed of what we were doing and the CG too. In many cases, it was necessary to get a legal officer to approve.

Meanwhile, a professional photographer showed up one day on very short notice. He wanted to take photos of Parris Island and recruits. The photographer brought along a "coffee table" book of his previous photographs. He planned to take the photos, publish them in a similar book, and sell the books.

Since he was doing this for profit, I had to write a Letter of Instruction (LOI) which had to be approved by base legal. I had my assistant write it and print it.

Many legal officers or military attorneys are great, can-do officers. Others just see litigation risk everywhere they look, around every corner and under every stone, just like in corporate America. They prevent good things from happening along with bad things.

I believed that there was no harm in accommodating this photographer. His books were in good taste and we would control where he went and what he got to shoot. Besides, if glossy books of photographs of Parris Island ended up on a few coffee tables around America that is a good thing.

I was going to walk this through personally so that the photographer could get started with his work. I called the Law Center to ask for the attorney I normally worked with. He wasn't there.

The one legal officer who was there was a guy who I knew would look for reasons to deny this photographer's request.

It is always easier to say no from behind the safety of a phone call or e-mail. I decided to remove that safety. He outranked me, so there was a little bit of a risk, but I did it anyway.

I took the photographer's coffee table book and the photographer himself to the Law Center. We walked down the hall to the legal officer's office. I knocked on the door, smiled, walked in his office and shook his hand.

"Sir, I've got great news! This renowned photographer has come to Parris Island to shoot photos. He is only available for one day and on short notice, so forgive me if I did not route this normally! This is a rare chance to have our lovely base showcased in such beautiful and graphic detail! I just had to come here personally and show you this beautiful book he created! In fact, I even brought the photographer himself! It is my pleasure to introduce you to John. In fact, I'll even bet that he will send you a signed copy of the book when it is complete!"

The lieutenant colonel uneasily rose to shake the photographer's hand.

"Check out this book, sir! Wow! I wish I could take photos like this. Maybe he could teach my combat correspondents a few new techniques! Will you do that, John? Sir, since we are already here together, let me just get your signature on this LOI real quick and we'll get to work."

"Ummmm...well, I ummm, ok, sure", said the legal officer. He signed it.

I thanked him and we left his office. Then, I heard, "Jim, come back here please."

He told me that he did not feel comfortable signing off on it and normally wanted more time to think it over.

But just this one time, he could go along. But please don't come back here like this again.

"Aye, sir...I understand."

The photographer and I left the building, looked at each other and laughed.

Keys to Triumph

1. Choose battles carefully. This one was worth it.
2. People have a much harder time denying you when face to face with you. There is no substitute for conducting business in person. Your chances of success increase tremendously.
3. Your passion and enthusiasm must be greater than the obstructionist tendencies of others.

Chapter 10 "The Cocktail Party 9/11 Campaign"

In December, 2001, three months after the terrorist attacks in New York City and Washington, D.C., I was in Tampa, FL visiting family for the Christmas holidays. I attended a cocktail party and was approached by a well-dressed, middle-aged, but old-moneyed man I knew to be living well from the proceeds of a trust fund.

He made small talk with me about the military, the recent start of war in Afghanistan, and terrorism. Then, without a hint of humor he said, "Well, James, now that we have been attacked, recruiting must have picked up. I guess you guys don't have to work so hard to recruit high school dropouts and felons these days."

Clearly, he intended the remark as an insult to the military and everyone who considers joining or who joins and serves.

Haughty attitudes like this come from a place of deep personal insecurity that wears an ostensibly sophisticated mask.

However, authentic sophistication never judges or insults service members or other public servants. In fact, authentic sophistication disregards stereotypes and looks deeper than what meets the eye with all people.

"The Dress Blues Test"

A military uniform presents an interesting test. Some people react with indifference, some with hostility, and some with disdain. Generally speaking, I am happy to say that the normal reaction is one of respect.

I had once heard of a "dress blues test" in Marine Corps recruiting parlance. In other words, how do people react to the sight of a Marine in dress blues? Is it a reaction of indifference, hostility, disdain, or respect?

We were targeting recruiting dollars for advertising at demographics of people most likely to enlist, and it should not be any other way. Our public affairs efforts were often designed to complement the recruiting effort. We were spending plenty of time, effort and expense talking to people who already respected the blues.

The man at the party unconsciously gave me a message between the lines. It was time to start talking to people like HIM. Why were we not talking to his demographic? It was time to start talking to people who were indifferent, hostile, or disdainful toward the blues. I started to ask myself how we could use the media to talk to him and to people like him.

I began to think of suitable criteria. For this campaign, I wanted well-respected big-city or national media that typically reached an educated or upscale demographic. A reputation for liberal bias was even better.

When I returned to Parris Island, I had a conversation about it with our commanding general and chief of staff. I told them that as a result of this encounter, I wanted to pitch national media that is normally read, listened to, or viewed by his demographic. I wanted to invite them to send reporters to Parris Island to cover boot camp for a few days, and that recruiting and training new Marines during a time of war was certainly newsworthy. They were supportive.

In October, about one month after the attacks, I was in New York City where we visited several major media outlets. While there, I had a conversation with a senior editor at *The New York Times*. He made an interesting admission; that the paper was often focused on Pentagon or high-level service or Defense Secretary-level reporting. He felt that such a focus on defense policy came at the expense of reporting on the troops, the everyday existence of the military men and women actually fighting wars.

I replied that most national media had a similar focus on policy and defense politics, but that the troops were a rich and never-ending source of interesting stories.

Local media is always interested in covering stories about local military people and local bases. A local reporter or editor is normally very interested in a local tie to a national or international story, and a war certainly qualifies. A deployment of a unit is always of interest to local media, especially a National Guard or reserve unit (civilians from the community who are members of the Guard or reserve can get mobilized into active service in the event of war or national emergency).

Even if there is no war or national emergency, reporters from local media markets of all sizes visited Parris Island every week to document the human interest side of boot camp. So, for example, if a television news station from Birmingham, Alabama came to visit us, they typically asked us if we could make recruits from Birmingham available for interviews. We always accommodated such requests. Not only does the public have a right to know what we were doing, but the stories helped the recruiting effort there.

I never saw any reason why national or international media could not cover stories in a similar way. My conversation with *The New York Times* editor confirmed it.

So, I began calling national media. The 9/11 terrorist attacks brought fresh interest to our mission at Parris Island. For example, ABC News did a New Year's Eve story of celebrations around the world. They sent reporters to cover young people ringing in New Years Day 2002 around the world in cities such as Rio de Janiero, New York City, Paris, Los Angeles, and others. They also sent reporters to Parris Island. I spent that evening with recruits and an ABC News reporter, producer, and a cameraman. The story here was the contrast. Young people partying on New Year's Eve compared with young people at Parris Island voluntarily undergoing Marine Corps boot camp while our country was at war.

I called C-SPAN, the private, nonprofit network that televises many federal government proceedings as well as public affairs programming. The latter often includes interviews with elected officials or agency heads, and some defense reporting. It also includes tours of sites of historical significance, and lectures on subjects ranging from historical figures (such as U.S. presidents) to current and historical events, and books.

The public affairs programming is generally in-depth and in my opinion, is usually of scholarly quality. Viewer demographics in recent years, according to Hart Research, showed that about 47 million adults watch C-SPAN regularly. About half are college graduates and 28% of 18-49 year olds report watching the network at least once per week. So do 19% of 50-64 year olds and 22% of viewers over the age of 65.

I pitched them. At first, they were not interested. They were focused on defense policy and events in Afghanistan. I replied that troops in the field and developments there was certainly of intense public interest. However, I asked them if they felt that it was compelling that young people were enlisting in a time of war. I offered them an opportunity to talk to young recruits in our recruiting pipeline and ask them about their personal motivations for serving before they arrived at Parris Island. I offered them access to the same recruits after they arrived here.

It took several months of constructively persistent "stalking", but C-SPAN eventually sent a crew to Parris Island and produced a positive show.

I asked for and received support from the Pentagon for these stories. I also pitched the Washington Post, who sent a reporter. Between the Washington Post and C-SPAN, we exposed the Parris Island story to millions of educated men and women. The Marine Corps needs the help of influencers like any other organization, and those two media organizations were exactly what I was looking for.

Remember, it does not necessarily take millions of people. If the story is viewed or read by one person who is well-positioned to help, sometimes that is all that is needed. It could be one powerful senator with influence over the defense budget. It could be one student with a sense of patriotism and adventure who is on the fence about serving. It could be one university president deciding whether or not to support Reserve Officers Training Corps (ROTC) on campus.

It is impossible to know exactly what impact these stories had, but they certainly did not hurt.

It all started with one rude comment at a cocktail party, and the man who uttered it inadvertently did us and his country a favor. In public relations, business and in life, I have learned to regard such people like a memo pad, reminding me of something I may need to do. With one comment, he revealed an opportunity and provided motivation for a public affairs campaign to educate him and a few million of his peers.

Perhaps gratitude is in order.

Key to Triumph:

1. *Something you need is often hidden within something you may not like*. Opportunity really is everywhere. It is fleeting, it may be disguised as adversity or pain, but it is everywhere.

2. The more engaged you are with what you do, the quicker you will be to recognize opportunity. The more opportunities you recognize, the more you can seize. The more opportunities you can seize, the more they multiply.

Chapter 11 "Don't Ask, Don't Tell" at Boot Camp

The nation's policies concerning gays and lesbians serving in the military have changed over recent decades. Previously, anyone who was gay or lesbian or had engaged in homosexual conduct was barred from joining the armed services.

Under President Clinton, the policy was changed to, "don't ask, don't tell" (DADT). The policy prohibited people from serving who "demonstrate a propensity or intent to engage in homosexual acts" from serving in the armed forces of the United States, because their presence "would create an unacceptable risk to the high standards of morale, good order and discipline, and unit cohesion that are the essence of military capability" (Title 10, United States Code, Section 654). The law was in effect from early 1994 until it was repealed in 2011 and gays and lesbians could then serve openly.

DADT prohibited any homosexual or bisexual person from disclosing his or her sexual orientation or from speaking about any homosexual relationships, including marriages or other family attributes, while serving in the United States military. The act stated that service members who disclose that they are homosexual or engage in homosexual conduct should be separated (discharged) except when it "would not be in the best interest of the armed forces" or a service member's conduct was "for the purpose of avoiding or terminating military service."

The last sentence in the last paragraph was a source of constant difficulties. The first four weeks of Marine Corps boot camp are a culture shock. Out of all of the stress and mayhem, many recruits emerge as special cases who feel as though they made a mistake by enlisting and will do almost anything to get out. There are plenty of stories of these kids committing crimes, running away in the middle of the night, attempting suicide or threatening to kill themselves if they can't go home. Many of them would claim to be gay in order to get sent home.

Under DADT, every such claim had to be investigated. After all, in DADT the DT means, "don't tell" and they told. We had to determine if they were actually gay before processing them for discharge. So, an officer had to be appointed to conduct the investigation. It was usually a junior officer such as a lieutenant or captain, normally a series commander.

I cannot remember a single officer, myself included, who enjoyed conducting these investigations. Personally, I thought they were demeaning. There were a thousand things I would rather do than run around like *Sherlock Holmes* or *Magnum P.I.* trying to determine if a kid was gay or just trying to play us so that he could get out of his enlistment.

So, we asked his drill instructors if he had engaged in homosexual conduct or expressed a willingness to engage in homosexual conduct. Then, we had to ask other recruits that were in close proximity to him if he had engaged in homosexual conduct or expressed a willingness to engage in homosexual conduct.

"Have you ever seen him sexually aroused in the shower room?"

Then, we had to do some independent verification. One officer took it too far when investigating one recruit's claim. He called people that the kid had known: high school teachers, coaches, classmates, Boy Scout troop leaders, and even his pastor, asking if the kid was gay. The problem was that the recruit came from a town with a population of about 5,000. You can imagine how fast word travels in a small town, and so he did not exactly receive a hero's welcome after his four-week enlistment.

That resulted in some changes. The rules were relaxed and these investigations were subject to more supervision from legal staff. However, there was always a lot of attention on the issue.

I did not enjoy this issue as a series commander. I did not enjoy this issue as a public affairs officer. As a controversial issue, much of what was published about it and attributed to us was going to offend someone.

We could keep it sanitized by simply stating the law and parroting talking points such as, "we are committed to implementing existing defense policy and U.S. law." That is always the safe course of action, but it does not satisfy an aggressive reporter looking to stoke debate.

I did not enjoy the issue. On the other hand, the media loved this issue. It had many of the elements of news: conflict, controversy, currency, prominence, significance, and of course, sex.

The *newspaper sales test* is simple. The more of the elements of news, the more newspapers it sells. This story sold newspapers.

The DADT Ambush

A reporter from the *Louisville Eccentric Observer* visited Parris Island. The *LEO*, as it is known, is a weekly alternative newspaper. Alternative newspapers such as this do not provide comprehensive coverage of general news. Instead, the reporting is stylized and often features investigations into topics that are edgy. A major focus is feature articles of local culture and people, especially nightlife. Coverage is locally focused and geared toward younger urban readers. Other examples of newspapers of this genre are the *Village Voice* and *Creative Loafing*, also known as *CL*.

There was a benefit to the recruiting effort to gain coverage in alternative publications. Our target market reads those newspapers, too. However, I had read enough of them to know that they provided much coverage of lesbian, gay, bisexual, and transgender (LGBT) issues and the LGBT community.

I gave the reporter a standard tour of the base, explaining each phase and activity of recruit training. I described what they were and the purpose of it. I arranged interviews for him with recruits from his market which was Louisville, KY.

Toward the end of the visit, he asked me if I could arrange an interview with the commanding general.

I asked him what he planned to ask the general. He replied that the interview would cover two areas. He wanted the general's insights on recruiting people in a time of economic prosperity and the drawdown of combat operations in the Balkans. Was recruiting a challenge? The second area covered was the training of young people. He wanted to find out about attitudes of young people fresh out of high school toward serving their country (this was in 2000). Were young people still patriotic? What motivated them? Was there a common theme?

I asked him if there was anything else that he wanted to talk to the general about. He said there was nothing else. I asked him if he was sure. He said yes.

I went to the general's office and he agreed to the interview. Next, I wanted to prepare him by telling him what the interview would cover, according to what the reporter told me. The general was skeptical that someone from an alternative weekly paper would stick to a "script" but we went forward anyway.

The interview took place in a conference room with the general at the head of the table, the reporter to his left, and me to the left of the reporter. The reporter turned on his recorder and started the interview.

"Thank you for agreeing to this interview. So, General, why is it that just because someone is gay they cannot be good Marines?"

The general glanced my way. I shook my head and tried to interrupt, looking for a quick recovery. But the general told me and the reporter that it was okay. He answered that it was his responsibility to ensure that the spirit and letter of the policy was followed, and if society ever reached a place where the American people were comfortable with gays and lesbians serving openly, we would adjust and accommodate.

The reporter then proceeded as he had said he would with questions about recruiting and training. The interview took approximately 10 minutes.

It was now the end of what had been a long day. We got in the van and the reporter asked me to take him back to his hotel. No, I told him. First, I needed to show him something.

But he was tired, he said. Tough! He ambushed my General and me with the DADT angle, and did not seem interested in our realities. It was time to show him our realities.

He was doing his job for his newspaper and readers by addressing DADT. However, some context was needed.

I pulled up to a recruit barracks (building where Marines or recruits live) that was empty and told him to get his camera and follow me inside.

The recruits spend their time at Parris Island in barracks, when not in the field. They live in a large concrete room called a squad bay. The walls (bulkheads in naval terminology) are concrete, as are the floors (decks in naval terminology) and the ceiling (overhead in naval terminology). The capacity of each squad bay is one platoon with a maximum of 88 recruits. They sleep in metal bunk beds (racks in naval terminology). There is no privacy in the squad bay.

There is no privacy in the bath and shower facility (head in naval terminology) either. The toilets are lined up and have partitions to divide them into stalls, but no doors. The shower room is small, offers shower faucets and shower heads but no partitioning or privacy.

These barracks were constructed in the 1950's and 1960's and were in use then and still are.

I took the reporter on a tour of a squad bay so that he could see for himself where recruits lived while undergoing recruit training. I wanted him to see the openness and austerity of it, and the utter lack of privacy. It is not unlike a medium or minimum security prison.

Finally, I took him into the shower room. I told him to imagine 88 young men using this small shower room at the same time. Then, I asked him if he had a son. He said yes. I told him to imagine if his son enlisted and came here and lived right here in a squad bay like this one. Then, I asked him to imagine his son living in such close quarters or using this small shower room with someone who is openly gay. I asked him if that would be okay with him. He told me he had not really thought of it that way and he understood our perspective.

I had to make it visual, and so he needed to experience the look and feel of the squad bay. The reporter himself was not a veteran and so this debate about gays in the military was just academic to him. However, it was not academic to us. At the time, DADT was the law. There were no openly gay or lesbian service members and the squad bay provided a great visual reminder of the reason for it.

The prevailing (and completely unscientific) opinion among many of us was that the law was cumbersome to implement (through those investigations) but that the law seemed like a sensible way to avoid interpersonal conflict among service members. I always think of that squad bay (or close quarters on naval vessels or any other military workplaces) and whether or not everyone can set aside such differences when in combat. Of course people can. They must.

I can't speculate how that might work in every human interaction. I can't speculate on the personal discipline of everyone in any given situation where you mix openly gay or lesbian people in close intimate quarters with people who are not gay or lesbian.

DADT was repealed, and the military just adjusted to the change as always. They salute, do as ordered, and make it work.

Observations:

1. If a reporter asks for an interview and you grant it, be prepared for any direction the interview may take, despite the reporter's assurances.
2. Know the reporter and the media outlet they come from and prepare accordingly.
3. Don't miss an opportunity to make something visual. Visual makes it simple.

Chapter 12 Red Light Means Stop!

Parris Island generally has on average about 600 drill instructors training recruits at any given time. At the recruit depot in San Diego, the number is roughly the same, so there are on average about 1200 Marines serving on drill instructor duty at the two recruit depots. While many of them are exemplary Marines, some of them stand out even further.

I had one who had worked for me during my time as a series commander who was nominated for Drill Instructor of the Year. In fact, I wrote a large part of the nomination citation personally. He went before a couple of screening boards and was selected as the only one from all of Parris Island's drill instructors to go to Washington D.C. for a recognition ceremony.

He deserved it and had exactly what we were looking for. As a senior drill instructor (SDI), he demanded very high levels of performance both from recruits and other DIs, leading by example from the front. His platoons of recruits consistently exceeded Parris Island averages in academics, physical training, and drill. When I interviewed our recruits that were under his charge, I heard from them time and time again that they were trained hard by this man, but were doing well under his leadership and mentoring. Some of them told me that they regarded him as a father figure. Others told me that they wanted to quit, but he persuaded them not to. There was one who had threatened suicide by climbing onto a ledge of the third story of the barracks and threatening to jump. He literally talked that kid off the ledge.

So, I called some news media and invited them to profile him. A television reporter accepted my invitation and came out by herself with her camera and equipment.

We met at the rifle range where his recruits were undergoing the first week of marksmanship training. It is known as "grass week" because the recruits sit in a grassy field and practice shooting positions (sitting, kneeling, prone, and offhand, also known as standing). No ammunition is issued and there is no firing. All of the other DIs assigned to the recruits' platoons are present and provide supervision, along with marksmanship coaches and instructors.

She attached a lavalier microphone to his collar which was wired to a radio transmitter clipped to his belt for his interview. A lavalier is a small microphone and whatever is said into it is routed directly to a recording device via the radio transmitter. It can also be routed to a speaker on the camera itself.

She interviewed him for a few minutes about the recognition he had achieved, what he was doing, and what made him different as a drill instructor. It was a positive interview. Then, she asked me if she could take her camera and move among the recruits to get some footage of them. I said yes.

She mounted the camera on her shoulder, walked away, and began doing that. My cell phone rang and I took it, so I got distracted.

It was at about that time that some other DIs came up to the SDI that had just been interviewed and asked him how it went, what it was about, etc.

Then, these guys began an enthusiastic conversation about the reporter herself, particularly her ass.

After nearly a minute of discussing shape, size, roundness, and firmness, they realized that the SDI still had the microphone on, with the red indicator light on the transmitter still on. Every word of the conversation was recorded. The last words recorded were, "Oh shit" followed by sounds of fumbling before the transmitter was turned off.

The fun was over. She finished her work, thanked us and left. I normally stay in touch with reporters while they work on stories. I called her a couple of times throughout the day to ask when the story would be on the air. Her short responses were a pretty good indicator of her mood, which was icy and I knew why. I tried to address the elephant in the room directly, but was met with, "I gotta go."

This was pretty much unsalvageable. The story did not run, and the entire base was in the doghouse with this TV station for a while.

Drill instructors and military people in general normally possess a higher than average degree of *situational awareness*. Situational awareness is perception of the environment around you, a heightened sense of people, things and events nearby.

Average people lack situational awareness, and you can see this in everyday life. Think of someone on the road, driving along in the passing lane abreast of other drivers, at the same speed, preventing passing, and slowing traffic and unaware of others who want to pass. Think of a guy who, because of his booming stereo, does not notice the ambulance or fire truck with lights and sirens behind them. At the grocery store, someone absentmindedly blocks an entire aisle with her cart.

There is a time and place for guy talk. There is a time and place for girl talk.

Lapses in situational awareness, even momentary, can be disastrous. Think auto accidents, plane crashes, and now this story which should have been positive.

It is easy to get comfortable with reporters. But don't drop your guard.

Once, I was walking with a reporter and cameraman that I had spent several days with. It was at the end of the day after we had just about finished our work. Then, in a friendly conversational tone, the reporter asked me for my personal opinion on gays in the military, which has always been controversial. I was about to answer when I noticed the cameraman swinging the lens slightly in my direction. The red indicator light was on.

Moral of the story

1. When it comes to reporters, *there is no such thing as "off the record"* especially when recording devices are nearby.
2. If you see a red light that is lit on any sort of camera, microphone or any recording device, don't say anything that you do not want to be public. Anything you have said when it is on is now out of your control.
3. Situational awareness...always.

Chapter 13 Grand Stagecraft-A Presidential Visit

In March, 2003, the U.S. commenced war with Iraq with a long-anticipated invasion. I was at Camp Lejeune, NC at the time assigned as a public affairs officer.

Camp Lejeune is a major Marine Corps base with an amphibious warfare mission. It is located just north of Wilmington and is a 246 square mile base with 14 miles of beaches, ideal for training for amphibious assaults.

Amphibious warfare is a traditional Marine Corps mission and is carried out by land and sea, or naval forces together. Marines can invade a country from the sea, embarked aboard naval vessels. The invasion can be carried out using specially made armored vessels launched from naval vessels. Aircraft is also used, normally a combination of attack helicopters, transport helicopters, and fixed wing fighter or attack planes.

Naval gunfire and aviation supports such missions as well.

Tens of thousands of Marines took part in the invasion of Iraq, and many came from Camp Lejeune. Pre-deployment activity and security was high, and so was media interest. Several Camp Lejeune Marines were killed in action during the early stages of the war, and in late March, we received word that **President George W. Bush** was coming to Camp Lejeune. A White House Press Corps detail was assembled and I was assigned to it.

There was much to coordinate, and it had to be done flawlessly. President Bush was going to visit on April 3 and deliver a speech. Then, he was scheduled to meet with Marines and their families and depart.

For the speech, Marine Corps engineers constructed a temporary stadium from wood. The stadium was set in a large grass field often used for parades. It was adjacent to a field house athletic complex and a small chapel.

Access to the base was an issue for anyone without a military identification card. Security was the foremost concern, and traffic flow had to account for the security.

There are always issues with protocol in the military, and in the highest levels of the government. This was certainly evident in discussions over seating charts. Local officials were invited aboard Camp Lejeune to hear the speech, and when they were mixed with senior officers and civilians from the Defense Department, the self-importance, jockeying and rank-pulling on display was predictable. "I must be placed closer to the president because I am senior." There will always be somebody making demands prefaced by, "Don't you know who I am?"

I also attended a meeting about the speech that President Bush was going to deliver. We were asked to submit names of people that could be included into the speech that would be loaded into the teleprompter for the president to read. The names were people who would be thanked for various contributions or recognized for various achievements. I was struck by how easy it seemed to get a name just written into the speech. I probably could have submitted my mother's name, your dog's name, your name or even my own.

We wrote and issued press releases. They were nothing glamorous, just information for the media and the public announcing what time to arrive, where to go, the dress code, and to be sure to not bring weapons or glass aboard the base.

The logistical plan was for Air Force One to arrive at Marine Corps Air Station at Cherry Point, which is 46 miles from Camp Lejeune. There were support aircraft transporting the president's limousine and other vehicles to support the mission. The reporters of the White House Press Corps were to arrive in a chartered MD-80 passenger aircraft. VH-3D Sea King helicopters (designated Marine One when the president is aboard) would fly the president from Cherry Point to Camp Lejeune. Note that helicopters are plural. There are always three that fly together as a security measure. One transports the president and the other two serve as decoys.

I was tasked with ensuring that the White House Press Corps made it from Cherry Point to Camp Lejeune well in advance of the president arriving there, coordinating police escort off base and military police escort on the base. The reporters were in a chartered bus and I rode ahead of them with a North Carolina state trooper. The advantage of involving the troopers was that they could just activate their lights and clear traffic for us along the route. We arrived at the stadium and **Ari Fleischer**, the White House Press Secretary positioned the reporters.

The three presidential helicopters arrived and landed in an adjacent parking lot. The president was ushered to the stage on the stadium to polite but raucous applause from some 12,000 Marines and others in attendance.

He greeted everyone with enthusiasm.

"We really appreciate your welcome and we're proud to be with the Marines and sailors and families of Camp Lejeune. There's no finer sight, no finer sight, than to see 12,000 United States Marines and Corpsmen -- unless you happen to be a member of the Iraqi Republican Guard!"

There was much talk of the rapid progress of the invasion.

"Our Armed Services have performed brilliantly in Operation Iraqi Freedom. Moving a massive force over

200 miles of enemy territory in a matter of days is a superb achievement. Yet there is work ahead for our coalition, for the American Armed Forces, and for the United States Marines. Having traveled hundreds of miles, we will now go the last 200 yards."

When presidents deliver speeches, they always contain hints of something to come if not outright announcements of initiatives. You could dismiss the following as mere rhetorical flourish but it later proved not to be.

"People of this country take pride in your victories, and we share in your losses. Camp Lejeune has lost some good Marines. Every person who dies in the line of duty leaves a family that lives in grief."

When the president concluded the speech, he headed for a dining facility (commonly known as a mess hall or chow hall) to have lunch with some enlisted Marines. Of course we had to arrive first for some last minute advance work.

The place was sparkling clean and the young Marines who were slated to eat with the president and first lady were polite and extremely professional, but edgy. Enlisted Marines who are single eat free of charge in military dining facilities and officers pay a small charge ($3 at that time). Two lieutenant colonels were having a debate over whether or not to ask the president to pay when he arrived. One argued that it seemed petty and that he had a tight schedule, so let's just move him through. The other argued that the president receives per diem when he travels just like the rest of us, so he should pay just like the rest of us. I don't know who won that one.

Base dining facilities are not unlike some militarized Piccadilly Cafeteria. You show your identification card and just sign in if you rate free meals or pay if you don't rate the free meals. You stand in line and move through the serving line, then find a table and eat.

It was odd to see generals, a mayor, staffers, and two U.S. senators from North Carolina (**Elizabeth Dole** and **John Edwards**) just standing in line waiting to eat along with everyone else. Normally, these individuals are the center of attention anywhere they go, but they were just part of the crowd that day. The presence of Senator Edwards was somewhat noteworthy. He was a rags-to-riches multimillionaire trial attorney who had just been elected and was already receiving coverage and attention as a possible 2004 Democratic presidential candidate.

The senator was not particularly tall, slouched a little in posture, and kept brushing his hair aside with his fingers. He asked me to direct him to the "baahhthroom" in a soft, almost effeminate voice.

Meanwhile, the president was moving among Marines, greeting them. He sat down at a table for four with the first lady and two young Marines and started eating with them. A few reporters asked me for the names of some of the Marines there, especially the two that were eating with the president. I moved toward the president's table to try to get the names, but a secret service agent stopped me. I explained what I was doing, and then the agent himself got the names for me. President Bush looked up, saw me and smiled and waved. Otherwise, I had no personal interaction with him.

We left the dining facility and headed back to the stadium and field house. There was a chapel near the field house, and some family members of Marines were gathered inside the chapel. The family members were of Marines who had been killed in action within the last three weeks.

President Bush was entering the chapel to visit them personally and privately.

Ari Fleischer had talked to me about this earlier in the day, and we were ordered to keep all reporters as far away from this as possible. I understand why.

The emotions of loss were extremely raw and fresh and the interaction between the president and these people was intended to be personal and on a human level, not for public consumption.

On the president's orders, these Marines had died in combat and he had come to visit their surviving families. He said to them, in essence, "I ordered him into combat and he is now dead. I am here to mourn the loss with you, to answer your questions, and to make sure that you are taken care of."

That could not have been easy. President Bush felt that publicity and politics had no place here. Throughout his time as president, he did this regularly but it was almost never reported. At the end of his presidency, he looked aged like all presidents do after the strain of the job. In his case, I could see why. I am certain that those years of submitting himself to face the human costs of his actions as commander in chief took a toll.

The reporters that were with us gave us no trouble. Nobody tried to sneak over to the chapel with a camera to "get that exclusive." There was some reporting of it on CNN, but it was not extensive and there was never any proactive effort to let media know that it was happening.

The president then boarded Marine One and left Camp Lejeune.

Observations

1. There are events that are closely planned and choreographed for public consumption. There are just as many events that are closely planned and choreographed that are NOT meant to be seen. That is government. In a free country with a free press, you should always be prepared for things to be seen that are not intended to be.

2. Things are almost never quite as they seem. A great deal of politics is stagecraft, and the U.S. president is the ultimate political celebrity in our culture. As such, the president is a constant fixture in the lives of people in our country and around the world, no matter who holds the office. Everybody views the president in terms of their own likes and dislikes. There is no public

affairs effort that will make everyone approve of or like the president.

3. In this case, the event was big and public and not easily influenced by "spin". The press just showed up and reported on the speech (which was provided to them) and the surrounding events. The public affairs effort that day was more or less logistical in nature; a lot of "traffic management."

4. President Bush frequently visited families of service members killed in action. He also visited service members who had been badly wounded or maimed in action. The White House did not publicize these encounters or deny them, willingly disregarding the politics of them. That is appropriate.

Chapter 14 Building a Business? Maybe the Media Can Help

Anybody who has ever started a business has stayed awake at night trying to come up with ways to find customers. Have you done this? Even better, you want the customers to find you.

We advertise, we network, we use social media, we answer proposals, and on and on, doing whatever it takes to build a following and customer base.

Advertising is great brand reinforcement. Large businesses spend fortunes to remind you everywhere you go of the lasting power and quality of their brand. An advertisement may not really convince you to buy, but it is meant to give you a touch; a reminder. So many touches, so many exposures, and then you may buy out of familiarity, comfort, or brand loyalty. For an example, look no further than your refrigerator and see your favorite beverages. How heavily advertised are they?

However, you don't have the advertising budget of Coca-Cola or Anheuser Busch, so what do you do? Has anyone benefitted from media coverage alone to boom their business? Of course!

As a great case study, let's go back to 2003, when the U.S. invaded Iraq.

American troops were provided with decks of playing cards with the names and faces of Iraq's "most wanted." The ace of spades was Saddam Hussein, with lower-ranking officials on the other cards.

The cards were actually designed by U.S. Army soldiers, and this clever method of identifying enemy most-wanted goes back as far as the Civil War. The cards were announced and shown to media by generals during press conferences.

One night, a Houston-based entrepreneur named Max Hodges was watching the news and saw the story. He found a high-resolution file containing the cards from a Department of Defense website and downloaded it. By the next day, the file had disappeared from the Defense Department website.

Now that Hodges had the file, he converted it to PDF and contracted the Gemaco Playing Card Company to print 1000 decks for $4000. In advance of receiving the printed cards from Gemaco, Hodges began selling decks of cards on amazon.com, eBay, and his personal website. The starting price was $4 per deck.

Meanwhile, the story of the cards was catching on, and the media was running story after story with images of the cards, footage of troops playing the cards, and military spokespeople and generals happily displaying the cards in combat-zone press conferences. The cards became a novelty item, and demand surged.
Hodges' $4 decks climbed in price over the next several days, reaching prices on eBay of over $120 per deck. Eventually, more sellers obtained images of the cards, produced and sold them, and the price dropped back down to a few dollars per deck.

Hodges grabbed the opportunity, and the U.S. military and the media did the rest. He was able to swim with the tide to huge profits.

This may have seemed like a stroke of genius, but it is nothing you can't do if you stay alert for situations that contain success opportunities. With the right mindset, you can see the possibilities when opportunity strikes. However, opportunity often shows up hidden in adversity, so fear keeps most people from recognizing it, much less acting on it.

Opportunity is elusive, but it exists everywhere. Not many people can spot it. If you love what you do, get skilled at what you do, elevate what you do to an art form, the opportunities will appear. You will just see them. It is that simple.

You might not be surfing the wave of a trend or quick fad like Max Hodges did, but that does not mean that media is not interested in you.

You just have to be alert for opportunities to showcase your business. Something is different about your business, and the trick is to connect it to what the media wants. Doing that means educating yourself on what is newsworthy from a reporter's point of view. The basics include, but are certainly not limited to proximity to power, local ties (in the case of local media), conflict, relevance to readership, and yes, scandal.

So, develop your skills at spotting and acting on opportunity, and extend it to finding ways to attract media attention. Do this, and you will quickly enhance your visibility, and likely your reputation and profits as well.

Chapter 15 If you are a startup, skip the gold-plated public relations firm and their gold-plated monthly bill.

Are you starting a business, and need capital and customers? Get a megaphone and get on the offensive. If you are an entrepreneur, you are playing offense.

However, many startup founders don't have a clue how to conduct a public relations effort, so they hire a PR firm to do it for them. I have worked with many of these firms, and the common business model is to charge a monthly retainer, normally five figures, with a commitment of at least three months.

Save your money and don't do it.

Most entrepreneurs start small and do everything on a shoestring, and a brand-name PR firm is an extravagance. Besides, it is unlikely that the same person who pitches you from the big firm will handle your account. More likely, your account will be handled by a junior account executive working on a salary of about $55,000 per year. You will not be her only client, and you will probably get about 15 hours per week from her. Don't expect your account to be a priority.

So, you can spend, say, $12,000 per month. That is $144,000 per year and in return, you may get half-assed work that costs the PR firm about $27,500 per year.

This scenario will not always be the case, and some firms will give you your money's worth. Many firms offer great research, ideas, and media contacts. Many PR professionals are former journalists, and know how to make you newsworthy. Coverage that tells your story in a way that attracts significant investment or sales justifies the effort and the expense.

Generally speaking, a small business startup should never pay $12,000 per month, or even half of that. Note that I said "small" business startup.

If you can't justify or afford the expense of the established PR firm, what can you do? Your business won't be built in a day, and even for $12,000 a month, your reputation in the media won't either. What is the best way?

There are the basics. You can position yourself and your expertise by setting up websites, exploiting social media, blogging, and making yourself available to reporters through a "push" or "pull" strategy. All PR is either a push or pull strategy.

Offensive PR is a "push" strategy. In other words, a firm shops your story around to media who might be willing to feature it, or responds in the event of media scrutiny to represent your perspective. A "pull" strategy is where reporters look for experts or quotes for stories they are writing. The PR firm positions you as an expert and connects you to the reporter.

One last tip: Test the responsiveness of the PR firm. If a PR professional is not responsive to your e-mails or calls for hours or days, it may be an indication on how they respond to reporters. Reporters are on deadlines, and if an hour goes by with no response, they will move on to another source. That other source could be your competitor. As an entrepreneur, you are looking to grab any success opportunity you can. Your PR firm should be nimble enough to grab them for you.

Chapter 16 Information is free. Shape it and benefit from it.

Maybe you have bought and sold stocks or mutual funds before. Have you ever hired a financial advisor? A couple of generations ago, financial advisors were called stockbrokers, and still are in some circles.

Stockbrokers once charged very large commissions for buying or selling stocks for customers. They did that because they could. The large firms, or wire houses, had the licenses, the technology, but most importantly, the research and the information that the rest of the investing public needed but did not have. The information advantage they had enabled them to mark up prices and set service charges at will.

Thanks to the internet and secure online trading, those customers gained the ability to research stocks online and make trades there too, so trading commissions shrank due to market pressure. As a result, nobody pays

$200 for a stock trade anymore. The industry had to change to an advice and relationship-based model. It used to be that the advice was free but the trade was not. Now the trade is free but the advice is not.

Information is freely available, so chances are that customers or potential customers have the ability to learn almost as much as you do about your business. Every business, every industry, every sector at every level is subject to it. Are you ready?

"The Loose Information Test"
1. Consider this litmus test. *When information is turned loose, does it help you or hurt you?* If it does not help, it is time to evolve your business model or practices, and perhaps employ a remedial public relations strategy.

I read about a businessman who was very active in politics and served in powerful positions on regulatory boards. However, he was known for being secretive and protective about rental properties he owned. Code inspectors and reporters descended upon the properties and found them to be deplorable, unfit for human habitation, and overpriced. Within one week of the story appearing in local media, he had to shut down his rentals, compensate the tenants, and resign from all of his public positions.

2. Protective, secretive tendencies will always make reporters curious, so don't set yourself up for disaster. *If you don't want it in the newspaper, don't do it.*

You will prosper personally and professionally when you connect yourself and your business with people instead of disconnecting from them.

3. Private triumph comes before public triumph. If you are conducting business in a way that you would be proud to tell your mother, your father, and your children about, chances are that you will enjoy a sound public reputation.

Ideally, creating and conducting business is a rich experience worth talking about. When your message finds its mark in some latent needs of people, your success stories will start mounting.

Chapter 17 Entrepreneurs can gain good public relations by just getting loose.

Entrepreneurs on tight budgets often assign a low priority to public relations (PR). Many startup business owners don't understand PR or think it is a frivolity, so they don't hire a firm to do it nor invest in the in-house talent to do it.

However, I must point out the obvious. What do you find to be more credible, a media story about a business or a paid advertisement about a business?

In a recent survey by BIGfrontier Communications Group in Chicago, 44% of the respondents who used PR outreach received funding in the one-to-three-month time period versus 14% of those that did not. PR is, of course, the craft of obtaining proper media coverage.

In the course of my business, I associate with many blue collar and white collar entrepreneurs. I find many of them to be possessed of leadership skills, energy, and optimism that are normally not found within layers of management in a large organization such as a corporation, university, or government. They have to have that type of life force because their livelihood depends on it; they don't get paid until they bring in sufficient revenue. However, the silver lining to that cloud is the freedom to say and do things their way. And nobody sells a story better or more passionately than an entrepreneur discussing their business concept.

So, if you are starting a business, just communicate your story to a reporter with the same fervor as if you are talking to a potential customer or investor at a chamber of commerce event. Unless you are starting a franchise (and have to work within the franchisor's media relations policies) or work in a heavily regulated industry, you have the freedom to express yourself however you choose. Here are some thoughts.

1. Go ahead and be your unfiltered self. Of course, common sense applies, but you are free to sell it your way. You control your message, and unlike a corporate or government communications scenario, you do not have to submit it through many layers of review. That means there is no committee of risk-averse attorneys and managers to water down your message to make it "safe." The content of your press release or other communications with the media can reflect your view of

your concept and yours alone. A qualified public relations firm can help.

2. Avoid overly formal, wordy press releases, and avoid industry jargon and acronyms. Acronyms are a lazy man's way of communicating. Nobody except the users of unique acronyms knows what they mean. The moment you use one that is not understood by your audience, you have lost your audience. Set yourself apart from your average or below average communicator by ditching the acronyms and taking just a little time to explain things in simple "Sesame Street" language.

3. Your audience is first the reporter, but ultimately it is readers in your target market. You are speaking to a large number of potential customers.

4. Position yourself as a thought leader. You know more about your concept than anyone, and you know what problems you can solve and for who better than anyone.

Finally, just be yourself, but be your best self. A good public relations firm can help you to do it right, say it right, and help you reach the right public.

Chapter 18 SEO Part 1: In your efforts to get noticed, be careful with content farms.

Search Engine Optimization (SEO) is a 21st century method of public relations, and it has become surprisingly effective. In short, SEO is the development of website visibility of a web page or website in a search engine's unpaid or "natural" search results. Since almost everyone researches on the internet now, search engines provide what the Yellow Pages did in past generations, with a far greater volume of information.

Good public relations through SEO means keeping up to date with the latest search engine algorithms, but the fundamentals will always remain the same. That means publishing content (articles, blogs, stories, etc.) that is useful and relevant, with links to other pages that are equally relevant and useful. This produces search engine results that last a long time, and are known as "white hat" SEO techniques.

For example, gaining favorable mention on a major, credible site with heavy traffic is an SEO jackpot.

This brings us to the content farms. A content farm is a publisher or company that generates large amounts of textual content in order to manipulate search engines and maximize website traffic to their sites. They do this to maximize advertising revenue based on a number of impressions, page views, visitors, etc.

They solicit articles, blog posts, quotes, etc. in exchange for appearing on their site. However, the quality of the site, audience, and advertisers may be suspicious. Sites that exist simply to game the search engines gain short term ad revenue but generate little value. If anything, their sites get quickly penalized or banned by the search engines.

Not all of them are bad. Some of them offer great forums, and they have a legitimate look and feel to them with recognizable advertisers and relevant articles and links. They organize their content into recognizable and easily understood categories, and the traffic is targeted and legitimate. They can offer real but inexpensive SEO and public relations benefits.

What do bad content farms look like? Here are some ways to recognize them:

1. Is the site looking for a source for an article, or just a cheap or free article (with no pre-screening of the author)? If they are looking for a cheap article, it is a red flag.
2. Look for lots and lots of ads, with little useful content.
3. Are the articles useful, with consistent themes throughout? Is the content original? If not, it is a red flag.
4. Are the articles commented on? Do they get shared on social media channels? If not, this is another red flag.
5. If a requestor sends you a fee schedule, they are not really interested in your quality as a source or subject matter expert. Legitimate bloggers and reporters are only interested in your quality as a source.

You can always search the site on Google or whichever search engine you prefer. Search the reporter or writer and the site itself. There is no substitute for your own gut instinct. If it looks like a site you would be proud to have your business associated with, then by all means, submit quotes or content to it!

Chapter 19 SEO Part 2: Your website will be rated, so optimize it constantly!

Small businesses and large businesses alike practice public relations through publishing blogs and articles. Such articles yield search engine optimization benefits if done right. Search engines such as Google have algorithms that reward usefulness. There is also a human factor involved.

You may or may not know that Google actually contracts companies to assign "utility ratings" to web pages. That's right! These companies employ armies of subcontractors who browse websites all day and rate them. A utility rating essentially evaluates search engine quality around the world by ranking and rating usefulness of websites according to language and location.

Highest quality or high quality ratings are assigned when a site has an obvious purpose and achieves that purpose very well. They are produced by people with a high level of expertise in the topic, and have a very satisfying amount of main content. The main content is prominent and easy to find. Supplementary content is helpful and contributes to a very satisfying user experience. The content as written displays a high level of professionalism. High-quality pages are associated with sites with recognized credibility.

A site will be rated low (slightly relevant or useless) and penalized if it contains spam. If content is created just for the purpose of putting ads on a page, or has no other purpose other than to get users to click on ads, it is considered spam. Spam is assigned a special quality of low rating. Thin affiliates also result in low ratings. A thin affiliate is a link that offers little additional information and no substantial value compared to other sites on the web or just has copied content from a merchant site. It appears to have no purpose except to generate commissions. Also keyword stuffing into an URL and "sneaky redirects" which redirect a user from one URL and domain to another URL and domain with spam intent. Others are pages that don't load, or results that contain unsolicited porn or foreign language. These are the sites that the search engines now rate very low and often ban.

Your public relations content on your site is under your control. Ensure that your content is professionally written, easy to find, and laid out well. Even if you must "give away" some good ideas, you have an opportunity to display expertise and thought leadership, and will gain a reputation as a resource. If you have affiliates or advertisers, the rule is simple. Choose affiliates and advertisers who are relevant to your business, complement you, and won't embarrass you.

Other simple but often overlooked suggestions for keyword usage include:

- Account for locale and culture. Remember that "football" means something different to a user in the U.S. than it does to a user in the U.K. or Australia. So does "bloody."

- Account for dominant interpretations. For example, if a user searches for "Apple," is the user looking for computers or fruit?

- Account for local intent. This is clear when a user is looking for something close and area-specific, such as, "what is the weather like today," or "where is a good Italian restaurant?"

- Account for changes in dominant interpretation over time. Imagine how the interpretation of the word "phone" has changed over a generation.

Well-selected keywords in a well-written article or blog entry are a highly economical form of PR. Cash-strapped startups with a website can and should blog like crazy to gain organic or natural search engine optimization.

SEO is not a pursuit known for glamour. However, smart SEO will raise your online profile. If you have an online presence, make no mistake, you are in the SEO business. If you are an entrepreneur in frantic growth mode, SEO is one of your best public relations weapons

.

Chapter 20 SEO Part 3: Create opportunities and find gold in the long tail!

When people search for you or your business on the internet, they use specific words such as your name or the name of your business. These keywords, if you will, about you are not common unless you are a household name or your business is. These long tail keywords account for the majority of search driven traffic.

Long tail keywords are the opposite of "head terms." Head terms are the popular and simple terms; the most frequently searched. For example, "grocery store" is a head term, but "organic foods in the Flint, Michigan area" is a long tail keyword or phrase.

It is a common search marketing error to look no further than head terms when developing a pay-per-click (PPC) advertising campaign or attempting to optimize content. However, the less-popular terms offer the best return on investment (ROI) because they are less expensive in a PPC campaign, and rank less competitively in organic search results. Furthermore, people who search using these terms generally know what they are looking for, are more qualified buyers, and are more likely to purchase.

There are many keyword suggestion tools. The most common is the Google Keyword Planner. Keyword planning tools return limited lists of the most popular keywords. So, keyword search tools can be helpful in showing a range of the mean or highest average of relevant keywords (the head terms). It is more than a standard deviation away from the mean to find terms that are specific to you, hence the term "long tail."

But if you are a smaller business fighting for search engine ranking and recognition in general, the long tail is where you will find your greatest opportunity. You will find the least expensive keywords in the long tail. If you can accurately assess which words are used to find a business like yours, you can create content on your site that will help you gain search optimization. Use the long tail keywords in your public relations efforts. Here are some ways to choose the right ones.

1. Get back to the fundamentals of who you are, why you are in business, and what is different about you. I repeat: get back to what is different about you. Your rewards in business and in life are based on your difference. Public relations are about telling the story of

that difference. Make sure that your content tells that difference.

2. If your business is locally based, make sure that the location or name of your city is emphasized throughout your content. If not, make sure that there is emphasis on "statewide," "nationwide," etc.

3. If there is anyone who is well-known who is associated with your business, make sure that person's name is included appropriately in your content. That applies to your name too if you want to promote yourself and your qualifications as an owner or principal.

4. Stress benefits more than features of your products or services in your content.

5. In media encounters, discuss benefits of your products and services, your differences, your qualifications and your brand name every opportunity you get. Create opportunities to do this, as good media coverage will provide greater SEO and publicity benefits than ad campaigns ever will.

Public relations for small businesses and entrepreneurs must do everything possible to ensure that your content and media coverage is optimized for search traffic. Furthermore, use the keywords in the content you control, such as your blog or website. Make sure your PR efforts tell the story of your specialization with the right keywords.

You will always find greater value and less competition in the long tail.

Chapter 21 Classic Public Relations. The Nature of News

Understand the nature of news in order to be newsworthy and get the sort of coverage you desire. As you strive to get noticed, your public relations effort will employ many tactics. You use social media, you write search-engine optimized (SEO) blogs and website copy, and you integrate all of this with your marketing and advertising efforts.

But the old school has always and will always get the best results. You can write optimized blogs until you are slap happy, but there is no substitute for a good article in a reputable, widely-read newspaper, magazine, or journal. That helps gain attention, which often feeds additional media interest.

The best way to accomplish this is to be newsworthy. The news has elements to it, and if your business has a story that has some of these elements, you may be able to gain a reporter's interest. These elements include, but are not limited to the following:

1. *Conflict*. If the story features a struggle between individuals, businesses, governments, or other institutions, it will attract a reporter's interest.
2. *Timeliness*. Unless it is a feature article, news must be very recent and fresh.
3. *Proximity*. Local reporters always look for local relevance to national or international stories. Offer them a local tie to a national story.
4. *Prominence*. It could be a story if it involves or is connected to a famous or notorious person or institution.
5. *Significance*. What impact will it have? The more people that are impacted, the greater value the story.
6. *Romance or adventure*. As a human interest feature, it is a good idea to highlight unusual or interesting things that people in your organization do.
7. *Sex*. It really does sell newspapers. On televised news, you don't have to wait long to see it, usually with pictures or footage under the pretext of being shocked or outraged by it.
8. *Progress*. Does the story continue with additional developments?
9. *Bizarre*. Unusual, unexpected, or freakish will move a story to the front page.
10. *Currency*. If it is an idea whose time has come, the matter will assume a life of its own. It will gain momentum in the media.
11. *Human interest*. This is an opportunity to highlight difference. It is a compelling side to someone's personal story.

Anything that you write that is placed in a place under your control, such as your website, your Facebook page, Twitter feed, etc. can say what you want. However, if you are looking for news coverage, the more of these elements the story has, the greater probability that you will gain the coverage. A qualified public relations firm can help.

Chapter 22 Classic Public Relations. Handle reporters the right way.

Reporters will try your patience and sanity. Deal with them properly and gain outsized and lasting benefits.

This is not complicated. If you are skilled in leadership and handling people with diplomacy and strength, you can emerge well from a media encounter, and the story will reflect it. If you are not skilled at these things, do some soul-searching and change yourself. Quality people and institutions will get positive media coverage. Why? Because they are worthy of it. The opposite is true as well. Time and time again, I have seen the best possible coverage in good or even negative events from observing these simple principles:

1. Be straightforward with reporters. Reporters are people too and sense if you are touchy, evasive, or overly protective of an area of sensitivity or secrecy.

This will only make them curious and press further there. Sometimes in public relations, it is necessary to tell a client that if they keep doing what they are doing, it will make them look bad because it is bad. There are ways to protect confidential and proprietary information. Do it right, and expect courteous and professional handling from the reporter. If you are covering up bad practices or wrongdoing, you will look like it and are asking for trouble.

2. *Reporters are on deadlines, so be quick to respond.* Since your very reputation is at stake, answering their questions must be your priority. Do not be too "busy" to respond to their inquiries. If you treat them like they are a nuisance, you deserve the public pain that is coming your way. You may not get many opportunities to make the news, so make the most of the opportunities you do get. If reporters find you easy to work with, it pays huge dividends.

3. *Be careful about bragging or exaggerating your virtues.* You should count on the reporter to thoroughly research your claims to independently verify them. Also, reporters tend to "comfort the afflicted and to afflict the comfortable" in their stories. It is a "Robin Hood" sort of ethic where they examine the rich or powerful and bring them down if warranted.

4. *If you have a situation that could become public, pre-empt it.* Doing so offers many advantages. Just as a fighter who throws the first punch can set the tone for the entire bout, you can start to define the story on your terms by simply speaking first. What sounds better? "Courageous whistleblower" or "Disgruntled

former employee?" Also, by giving a reporter an opportunity to break a story, you may have gained an ally.

A public relations professional should approach the job as though the media is a client, just as the paying client is. The PR person should do everything possible to facilitate smooth exchange between the reporter and the client, serving the needs of both. If you regard the media as an enemy, you are doing something wrong, in PR, in business, and likely in life too. The opposite is true. If you are adding value, doing it right, and have a story to tell, you need not fear the press. In fact, you should welcome and encourage their interest. A public relations effort is well worth the investment.

Chapter 23 Classic Public Relations. Take charge of how the public sees you.

If your business or life is in the public, it would be ideal if you were the subject to nothing but positive reporting. Public leadership will inevitably invite problems and criticism. Handle it properly and it is possible that you may come out stronger than before.

Previously, we have advised you to "be yourself," and allow the media to simply report on that. This is true if you are doing the right things and balancing everyone's best interests. If so, you can be reasonably confident that you will be subject to positive coverage.

But let's not oversimplify. Every person and entity you encounter is more complex and has more facets to them than meet the eye, just like you. You will look

different from every angle, and every perspective, and

to every person. Sometimes the differences in perspective are slight, sometimes they are vast.

Not everyone will give you credit for your good intentions or your good business practices. There is a rule of likeability which we are all subject to. Consider the following:

1. Approximately 25% of people will like you, and cannot be convinced not to like you.
2. Approximately 25% of people will like you, but could be convinced to not like you.
3. Approximately 25% of people will not like you, but could be convinced to like you.
4. Approximately 25% of people will not like you, and cannot be convinced to like you.

Even the greatest religious, spiritual, and political leaders the world has ever known were subject to this rule and were not well received everywhere they went. That applies to you too.

The first 25% are all for you and the last 25% never will be. Maximize your public relations efforts on the second and third 25%. Your public perception depends upon your ability to navigate the 50% in the vast middle. You can do that successfully by observing these principles:

1. Stay in your element. Imagine taking an eagle, clipping his wings, and putting him on display confined within a cage. How will he look? Well, he won't hunt or fly. He won't mate. He will become dependent on his captors for food. Would you release an eagle into a large city? Of course not, because he is completely out of place there too. It is only in his wild habitat that his natural genius and majesty becomes apparent. Your greatness will come out where it is allowed to, and you will get noticed for it. Identify your best habitat. Stay there, and you will flourish.

Where you are matters as much as *what* you are!

2. Always operate as though your private actions could become public knowledge. If you don't want it in the newspaper, don't do it. Conduct business in a way that balances everyone's best interests. It may not be appreciated by all, but it will not go unnoticed. *Private triumph comes before public triumph*.

3. Don't worry about critics. A critic is someone who feels inferior to you, and it usually shows.

4. Eagles soar above the flock of birds below and don't consult them for inspiration. In some way, you soar above the flock too and that is your opportunity to lead.

5. Handling miscommunications and misunderstandings is different in private than in public. *If you have a conflict with a person and want to resolve it, the answer is always more communication, not less*.

Not so with media. If a story does not reflect your point of view, you must address it with reporters in a disciplined and controlled fashion.

6. Turn problems into assets by addressing them in a lasting and honest way, and let your public know it when you do.

These are principles, but to put them into practice with the media, consult a qualified public relations firm. Your difference is among your greatest assets. Create situations where you can make maximum use of your assets and get noticed!

Chapter 24 Classic Public Relations. Fundamentals of Crisis Management.

Everybody blows it sometimes, though not everybody does so in a spectacularly public fashion. If you have received negative coverage, there are some principles that if adhered to, will minimize and repair damage to your public reputation.

It does not matter if you are the subject of one unfavorable story or many. You have your work cut out for you with the media and the public.

The worst thing you can do is to make reporters angry and curious at the same time; they will just dig further. If you have opponents or competitors, they will fill the information vacuum and define you. Do not hide behind a "no comment" and hope that it will all just go away. It won't.

The best thing you can do is to respond or even preempt it. Get to the bottom of the problem that is being exposed and make genuine changes. Bad press is painful. Regard the occasion as somewhat of a "memo pad." Prepare to set your ego aside. Altering your course is necessary, as the world is telling you, and the press and public will alert you to exactly how if you listen.

Bad coverage may be unfounded. You still have work to do.

You can never "spin" your way out of a history of willful bad practices. You can't hide them forever. The best way to repair a damaged reputation is to become worthy of a good reputation.

When it "hits the fan," you need to clean the fan, fix the fan, or replace the fan.

Principles of public relations crisis management

1. Resist combative instincts, and tell your staff to resist them too. The last thing you need to see on the evening news is footage of yourself or someone in your organization pushing a reporter, cursing at one, or extending a middle finger at a camera. Such *a reaction in one moment of emotional intensity WILL define you* in a way that is very hard to change.

2. Use direct communication with important publics. If you must go to the local chamber of commerce to explain yourself, do it. If you must approach government officials, do it. You may need to address it directly with your best customers. Whatever your most important publics are, *stepping up and addressing it forthrightly is the shortest route to reputation repair*. You may even find yourself in a stronger position when the problem passes.

3. Avoid the bunker mindset. Do not say "no comment" or refuse to respond. The public will view this as either cowardly, evasive, or both. Often, legal counsel will advise you to keep silent. They do this out of caution and to protect your position in the event of legal action. However, there is usually something you can say or do. Give the media something. There is a bigger picture that your attorney should recognize.

If your organization has created a damaging situation, err on the side of restoration. Doing so may actually prevent legal action from occurring, or minimize its effects. An attorney's world view is from a perspective of protecting a client in court. Everyone else's is based on self-interest and the public's is based largely on common sense. These world views are sometimes in conflict. A leader has to balance them.

4. Know when to use strict message discipline. When confronting hostile media, message discipline might be in order. Develop talking points and questions and answers (Q & A's) with help of legal counsel, public relations professionals, or other trusted members of your inner circle. If there is intense media interest, you can distribute a press release and Q & A's to reporters.

If they want a statement and you do not deviate from the release and Q & A's verbatim, that is strict message discipline. For example, the answer to every question might be, "we are investigating it fully and will decide what action to take once the investigation is complete." The advantage to this approach is that reporters will have no other quote from you other than what you have carefully chosen in advance. There will be no room to misquote you. All of the facts are not known right now, and that is fine. But when they are, make them available if requested. If you commit to provide the media with the results of an investigation when it is finished, you need to follow through as promised.

Strict message discipline is normally appropriate if criminal charges are pending. Avoid releasing someone's name to the media unless that person has actually been charged with a crime. Strict message discipline is also appropriate to protect a proprietary secret. Such secrets can include product formulas, business strategy, cost per unit, salaries, etc. Generally, media respects such boundaries, and such information is often protected by law anyway.

Strict message discipline is not necessary when releasing good news such as a new product or contract, charitable events or works, or anything an organization wants to showcase. If a reporter wants to write a feature on you or your organization, you should be welcoming, granting as much access as the reporter needs. Strict message discipline is certainly not needed for human interest stories.

5. If you have taken time to cultivate relationships with reporters, contact them to pre-empt a crisis or emergency event. Public relations are a relationship business like anything else. If you have worked with a reporter in the past and found that reporter to be balanced and professional, you should seriously consider reaching out.

Furthermore, understand a reporter's needs. They strive for professional advancement, and exclusive details, exclusive interviews, and exclusive stories help them. The news business is competitive and this is something you can use to your advantage. If you provide a reporter with something their competition does not have, they will remember it. Don't expect a "friend" in the press, but you can cultivate allies.

It works in reverse too. Reporters need you sometimes. While serving as the public affairs director at a large and famous Marine Corps base, we received many reporters on a weekly basis. I always had my office issue press releases to local media for events our commanding general wanted coverage for. Such events included parades, dignitary visits, demonstrations, concerts by the marching band, etc. There were some reporters and news outlets that were supportive and never failed to cover them. There were others that consistently ignored our press releases and follow up calls.

Many local reporters can be enjoyable to work with. They seem motivated by a genuine interest in community, and the people and institutions of the community. Such interest is reflected in their approach to reporting and in the stories they publish or produce. Others are not enjoyable to work with. They approach the job with a sense of professional entitlement bordering on arrogance. They interrupt, they ambush, they demand, and barge into places uninvited with cameras and microphones. You can spot them a mile away. At a press conference or news event, they are the ones fighting for position and even blocking cameras from competing news stations.

From time to time, unfortunately, Marines would commit crimes outside of the base. There were also incidents of sexual misconduct that media would catch wind of. There were incidents of death or serious injury to personnel, and there were many connections between our base and war in Afghanistan and Iraq.

All of these things resulted in intense media interest. The reporters that had taken time to cover our parades and concerts were reporters we had come to know and had a constructive relationship with. We knew they would treat us and our Marines fairly. They got the exclusives and the access they needed.

How about the ones who blew us off before? Predictably, they appeared and demanded details and access. Their demands were met with a faxed press release and some Q & A's, and little else. We hate to admit it, but on some level, we all play favorites.

6. Have a plan in advance. Your success is based on advance planning. Your competence will be on display. The competence of your staff will be on display. Your success will also be based on past successes and failures. In other words, your credibility will determine your success. It will also be based on relationships you already have with media.

Credibility is like money in the bank. Make deposits, and it draws interest. The more that is in the bank, the more interest earned. In fact, a good reputation can bring credit even when it is not actually warranted. A crisis can be a time to make withdrawals, but it can also be a time to make large deposits. That is done through decisive action and as much transparency as possible.

If you handle a crisis properly with the public and the media, you will earn MORE, not less credibility. That is the goal.

You never know when something bad can happen. Your fortunes can change direction on a dime. If you and your organization have your act together, you can be confident that you will emerge from a crisis with an intact reputation. A good public relations firm can help. Choose carefully.

Take time to assess yourself today. Take the *Investigative Reporter Test*. If an investigative reporter calls, would you be ready? Would you welcome them? If not, make the necessary changes.

If information about you is turned loose, does it help you or hurt you? If you don't want it in the newspaper, don't do it.

Private triumph always comes before public triumph.

Chapter 25 Journalism and Editing. If you want to be understood, stop doing this crap now!

"We want to talk right down to earth in a language that everybody here can easily understand." –Malcolm X

Consider these common examples of corporate-speak and military-speak:

"We are going to triangulate with Jim over in AP before moving forward."
"Our T & E is trending above plan for CY 2014."
"Utilize your SINCGARS for this week's field ex."

I have provided explanations of what these things mean.*Please read them before proceeding.

*Explanations of jargon and acronyms used:
Malcolm X (1925-1965) – civil rights leader.
Triangulate – Involving a third person in a conversation.
AP – Accounts Payable. Balances due a creditor for delivered goods or completed services.
T&E – Travel and Entertainment. Funds spent for travel or entertainment.
Trending above plan – Increasing past a budgeted or projected amount.
CY – Calendar Year.
Utilize – Use.
SINCGARS – Single Channel Ground and Airborne Radio System. SINCGARS is a radio communication system in wide use by U.S. and allied military forces.
Field ex – Field Exercise.

Now, let's talk about jargon and acronyms.
Jargon is specialized language. It is specialized for an industry or activity. For example, "touchdown" is specialized for scoring in football. It is also specialized for weather, describing where a tornado may land. It is also specialized for aviation, describing the point where an aircraft actually touches the ground when landing.

That is a simple example, but people who are engineers or information technology people have their own vocabulary too. Every industry and profession does. It may be something they use every day, but to others, it is unfamiliar.

Acronyms are specialized abbreviations. They are all around us. We all know what USA stands for. But we don't all know what OPEC is. It means Organization of

Petroleum Exporting Countries, which is a group of countries with large oil resources that collaborate on production and prices.

You must take time to help your audience or reader understand you. You must check for understanding when communicating about something specialized.

I met with an engineering firm owner who drastically needed to improve his sales. Together, we looked at his website. It was full of jargon and acronyms such as "VRS Portable System" and "Turnkey SCCT Enclosure." There were virtually no explanations of what these things were, what they did, or how they might benefit a buyer.

I have no clue what those things are. Many of his prospective customers probably don't, and there may be people who work with him who don't know either.

I had to explain to the man that if people were not sticking around to read the rest of the site, much less become customers, that it was HIS fault, not theirs.

It is not the job of your customers, your employees, your boss, your investors, or your audience to figure out what you mean without help from you. It is your duty to them to make it understood as easily as possible.

Have you ever read a book or report and realized that you reached the end of the page and could not remember what you read? If you did, it is because you went past a word or symbol that you did not understand. In fact, *the moment you go past a word or symbol that you don't understand, you go blank.*

Conversation works the same way. *As soon as someone utters a word or phrase that you don't understand, you tune out* while your mind tries to decipher something new and unfamiliar.

If you talk to people using jargon or acronyms that you know and they don't, you have lost your audience. You are talking in a way that is comfortable and familiar to you, but creating barriers to understanding for your audience.

If you use jargon or acronyms on your website, in an e-mail, in a press release, or anywhere else, you are going to lose most of your readers. You are a lot less likely to sell them anything if they don't understand you.

Do you get it now? I am going to say this in the strongest possible terms. Use of jargon and acronyms is a very lazy form of communication. Do you want to lose your reader because you were too lazy to take a few extra seconds to spell it out? SPELL IT OUT!

"If the orders are unclear, it is the commander's fault." – *The Art of War* by General Sun Tzu

During my years of military service, I have heard people of all ranks issue orders that were full of jargon and acronyms. Then, I would watch these same people express frustration when things went wrong, blaming "incompetence" or "poor training." It never dawned on them that their communication style just might be an issue and that they failed to make things clear.

If you are a leader, you must express yourself clearly. That applies to any setting or situation. Jargon is not clear prose. It is lazy, pompous and hollow communication.

If you speak using jargon or acronyms, you have no right to complain if your thoughts are not understood. You have no right to complain if your instructions are not carried out as you hoped. Even your employees may not understand. You could have someone working with you who is new to your business, but is afraid to ask questions out of fear of appearing ignorant.

If you use jargon and acronyms and actually expect to be understood, you suck as a communicator. And if you suck as a communicator, your effectiveness as a leader is quite limited. Consider yourself warned.

Jargon and acronyms are certainly fine in some circumstances. As long as you are certain that everyone that you are addressing understands you, then use them. Here are some guidelines to be a more effective communicator and leader:

1. If the voice in your head prompts you to check for understanding, then check for understanding. If your audience seems distracted or distant, that is a sign that you may need to check for understanding.

2. When writing, the rule for acronyms is to spell it out on first use, then you can use the acronym throughout. It is acceptable under Associated Press (AP) journalism guidelines to put the acronym in parentheses and then

to use the acronym throughout. The *AP Stylebook* is a helpful guide for acronyms and abbreviations.

3. Do not use jargon. Instead of saying, "This program is geared towards the end-user," say "This program was developed specifically for the needs of the customer." Train your suspicion to alert you if what you are saying or writing may not be quite clear. If you were hearing it for the first time, would it be clear to you?

4. If someone is speaking and they say something that you don't understand, stop them and ask for clarification. Same with written communication you receive. Ask for the answer.

5. Some acronyms are widely understood, such as TV, AM, PM, or USA. Generally, those do not require explanation.

6. Don't try to prove that you have good inside knowledge by using jargon or acronyms. It is likely to be viewed as a sign of poor communication skills. Do not use jargon in a press release, on a resume, on your website, your social media, your blog, or anything that is viewed by the public.

7. Do not use jargon or acronyms in a media interview.

Use plain English and full titles in business communication and always err on the side of total clarity.

Chapter 26 Journalism and Editing. Ditch the bad English. Literacy is an awesome weapon, so let's get proficient with it.

If you really want to get noticed, use literacy as a weapon. Develop this weapon every day. If that idea bores you, well then consider the benefits.

"Literacy is sexy!"

Someone who had a significant place in my life some years ago said that to me. I agree. Most people would agree with that statement. So, read on. I may be able to improve your love life by helping you to become a better writer. In order to do that, let's first take a look at some examples of writing that are decidedly not sexy.

- "IN THE FUTURE I WOULD APPRECIATE IT IF YOU STOP USING ALL CAPITAL LETTERS. IT IS TEXTUAL SCREAMING. IT COMES ACROSS AS PROVOCATIVE, CONFRONTATIONAL, AND VERY RUDE!!"

- "In journalism, the first sentence of a story is called a lead and should cover at least three of the following questions: who, what when, where, how, and why and the second sentence that comes right after it is called the bridge and it answers the two questions that were not covered by the lead, and so that is the lead and the bridge."*

*This sentence is painful to read because it is a *run-on sentence*. Generally, a run-on sentence has at least two independent clauses that are crushed together and not properly connected. Another rule of thumb in journalism is that it is a run-on sentence if it contains more than 30 words.

- "It is definitely an error, we combine what should be two sentences with a comma." *

*This is known as a *comma-splice*. I just took two independent clauses and connected them with a comma and a comma alone. When you use a comma to connect two independent clauses, make sure it is accompanied by a conjunction (and, but, for, nor, so, yet, nor).

- "I don't like it when James edits what I write. How dare he tell me that my grammar needs improvement? Citing sentence fragments." *

*A sentence must have a subject, a verb, and it must express a complete thought. If it does not, then it is a *sentence fragment*.

- "We do a lot of Editing and Writing for our Clients. However, there are times to Capitalize words within a Sentence and there are times not to do it. Our Clients call us to help them gain Publicity and help with Crisis Management. We also help them with Website Content that is done to the best possible seo and Journalism Standards." *

*Do not capitalize products or services offered. The rules for capitalization can be complicated, but most of us know *inappropriate capitalization* when we see it. This example is riddled with it. Also, search engine optimization (SEO) should be capitalized because it is an acronym, and unexplained acronyms are another no-no. The *Associated Press Stylebook* is a worthwhile investment as a simple guide for capitalization and writing in general.

These are some of the more common errors in website copy, newsletters, or other press releases that I have observed and had to fix. It is fine to be a "do it yourselfer," but you should have some mastery first.

I could change my own oil. When I was younger, I put my car on a ramp, slid under it, removed the plug from the oil pan, drained it, replaced the plug, removed the oil filter, and went to find a place to dispose of the used oil. Then, I replaced the filter and five quarts of fresh oil. It was messy, time consuming, and not much fun.

I could still do that. But why would I? For $39.95, I can sit in an air conditioned waiting room at an oil change place and read a magazine while the professionals do it in about 20 minutes. In fact, I would rather leave most engine maintenance to professionals. I don't really enjoy it.

If you are not a good writer, chances are you don't enjoy it much. If you are not a skilled writer and you write your own website content because you don't want to hire someone to do it, your website will look amateur. But hey, you saved money! Never mind the customers you lost because, well...they lost respect for the business after looking at a page or two of a poorly written site.

Be honest with yourself. If this is not something you do well, either learn to do it well or hire someone to do it for you.

Literacy is not just the ability to read and write at the elementary school level. Literacy refers to a degree of skill of writing, clarity of thought, and familiarity with literature of all kinds. We can all be literate, but if your literacy is of higher quality, more social, professional, and yes romantic doors will open for you.

The good news is that your literacy can be improved every day. You can work out every day and improve your physical fitness. Likewise, you can improve your literacy with consistent action and enjoy it.

1. The more active a reader you are, the better a writer you will become. That's right. Your mind will pick up skills in expressing yourself through the written word by observing how others do it.

2. Read something new every day. Turn off the TV and read instead, because your mind will retain information better if you read it instead of watching it. Read a newspaper or a book on something that interests you. You will become more conversant in that subject.

3. Reading makes you more conversant. The more subjects you are conversant in, the more literate you become. The more literate you become, the more interesting you become. The more interesting you become, the more people from all backgrounds want to be around you.

4. When reading, stop and take time to understand words, symbols, or concepts you do not understand. This is very important. If you are reading and you hit a word or symbol you do not understand, you will stop comprehending at that moment. That is why jargon and acronyms are such potent barriers to understanding. Don't use them and ask others not to use them. Stop and look something up if you don't understand it.

5. If you are writing and feel the slightest bit of uncertainty about proper grammar or sentence structure, take a moment to look it up. As previously stated, the *Associated Press Stylebook* is a good thing to own if you write regularly. Otherwise, thanks to search engines, the information you want is never far away.

6. Better writers become better speakers. The more you write, the better you will write, and your vocabulary will expand. The more your vocabulary expands the more polished you become at speaking.

7. Your word processor probably has a spelling and grammar check. Use it, okay?

Become more literate every day. It won't take long, and it will improve your life.

Chapter 27 Journalism and Editing. Stay out of court! Libel and other media law for beginners.

If you are going to start or sustain a public relations effort, there are some fundamentals to keep in mind, especially if it concerns the privacy or reputation of someone else.

If you are writing anything for public release, you must concern yourself with *libel*. *Libel is published or widely disseminated defamation. Defamation is a statement which is false that holds a person up to public contempt, ridicule, scorn, or hatred and holds his business or professional standing through fault. Slander is spoken defamation that is not widely disseminated.*

This is not intended as a substitute for legal advice. By all means, call an attorney or your legal team if something is unclear or touches on anything that could land you in court. Also, obtain legal help if you believe that your rights under these laws have been violated in the media.

It should be noted that there is no federal libel law. Each state has a slightly different law. Libel has five elements:

1. False. The statement is simply not true. The fact that a person has been quoted accurately is not a defense to libel if the quoted statement contains false information about someone. If it is opinion, it must be labeled as such and on the editorial page. However, if a comment cannot be proven as true or false, it is not protected as commentary.
2. Fault. In a civil suit alleging libel, the plaintiff must prove that the defendant was negligent or reckless-was at fault. Private citizens only have to prove that the person spreading the defamation was at fault. Public figures have a higher hurdle. People who voluntarily place themselves in the public eye must prove that the defendant acted with actual malice and disregard for the truth.
3. Published or broadcasted. It must be published or communicated to someone other than the person defamed.
4. Identification. Who was defamed must be identified, and names do not have to be used. For example, be cautious about speaking negatively and on the record

about a political party, business, or other entity.
5. Injury. Did the lie actually injure someone?

As stated before, the rules are slightly different for public figures. If someone is a well-known celebrity with a name that is a household word, that is a public figure or if someone is a vortex, or limited public figure, that means that someone has injected himself into a public debate in order to affect the outcome. With public figures, they must prove actual malice; that information was published with deliberate knowledge that the information was false: printed with reckless disregard for the truth.

Avoid libel with these nine steps:

1. Use official sources for criminal reports.
2. Never accuse someone of a crime. Using the word "alleged" is not a defense.
3. Get a legal opinion before publishing.
4. Don't attribute disease without evidence. For example, don't say that someone is HIV positive. Unless you are the person's doctor with permission to release it, don't do it.
5. Don't associate someone with a group that has a bad reputation. For example, a California court held in 1968 that it would be defamatory to say that someone is a member of the Ku Klux Klan.
6. Don't imply poor moral character.
7. Don't imply dishonesty or incompetence. State the facts and let the readers decide.
8. Avoid "red flag words" that are racist, sexist, homophobic, etc.
9. Retract when necessary.

Also, pay attention to the Privacy Act of 1974. This is a federal law that governs the collection, maintenance, and dissemination of personally identifying information that is maintained in records by U.S. government agencies. In other words, one agency with identifying information about you cannot disclose it to anyone else, even another government agency without written consent from you.

Exceptions are written into the law. Examples are uses associated with the census, law enforcement purposes, or congressional investigations.

This law protects you from reporters (or anyone else) accessing and publishing information about you such as income tax returns, military records, or other information about you that is stored at federal agencies without your consent.

In short, apply a simple test. The test is *who has a right to expect privacy?* States have privacy laws (however, there is no actual "right to privacy" in the Bill of Rights). You have a right to expect privacy in your home, for example. If someone takes pictures through your window and publishes them, they have invaded your privacy.

1. Private matters cannot be routinely published, even if what was printed is true. A person's privacy has been invaded if private facts about someone have been disclosed that are offensive and not newsworthy. However, public officials and public figures have little recognized privacy.

2. False light-placing a person in false light in the public eye (such as deceptive use of photos). When in doubt, get permission.
3. Appropriation-using someone's name or likeness for "advertising purposes" or "purposes of trade" without approval. Consent, however, is an absolute defense.
4. Intrusion-using hidden cameras or microphones where someone has a reasonable right to expect privacy.

If you publish or publicize something, you may or may not need permission to use someone else's work. *Copyright is the right of a writer, artist, composer, etc. to own, control, and profit from the production of his work*. However, not everything that is out there in the public is subject to copyright.

Nobody can copyright facts. Ideas cannot be subject to copyright, and neither can plans or titles. However, the way that these things are expressed may be subject to copyright. The United States Copyright Office is the definitive source for what is and what is not subject to copyright, whether published or not.

By the way, if something was published by a government agency it is in the *public domain*, and available for use. For example, if a government employee took a photograph that is used for an official purpose, you are free to use it.

In summary, be aware of libel, defamation, slander, privacy, and copyright. There is plenty more law and specifics regarding media, but these are major areas of concern.

Be very careful if any part of your public relations strategy involves publication of negative information about a competitor or opponent. If you publish anything negative, expect close scrutiny of your claims. If you can't defend it in court, don't do it, don't say it, or don't publish it. If you can't defend it to the public, don't do it, don't say it ,or don't publish it.

As stated before, if something is not clear then consult with legal counsel. If you are using a public relations firm or in-house public relations capability, then have them coordinate publicity efforts with your legal team. This is something that should be done anyway, especially if your industry is highly regulated.

If you are a practitioner of public relations, you must account for any unique legal position your client or employer has when planning publicity. If you are a leader or business owner using public relations, you must balance your legal position with your desired publicity.

There may be no conflict at all. If there is not, then you are doing something right.

References:
Associated Press Stylebook and Briefing on Media Law
Walsh, *Public Relations and the Law*
Bunnin and Beren, *The Writer's Legal Companion*
Sanford, *Synopsis of the Law of Libel and the Right of Privacy*

Chapter 28 Use public relations to raise capital-lots of capital!

If you are trying to raise capital, PR offers a chance to simplify your business for investors. However, the far greater impact comes from the credibility that media coverage offers, especially from a respected publication.

I conducted public relations for a startup financial services company. The CEO (chief executive officer), president, and other founders and leaders of this venture were experienced and accomplished entrepreneurs. Between them, they had started a community bank, an electronic trading network, a foreign currency exchange, and were licensed financial advisors and principals.

They created a new financial services company that would combine a global bank, wealth management, online securities trading, and a commercial finance company. As you might imagine, such a venture requires the founders to raise tens of millions of dollars in capital just to get the doors open. They had to get the doors open before they could even find the first client.

Such capital cannot be raised in small amounts from small investors. It takes too long. A *private placement offering* was the way to go. A private placement is the sale of securities (in this case, the securities are in the form of equity, or ownership in the company) to a select and small number of investors. Such investors might include mutual funds, hedge funds, pension funds, insurance companies, banks, and wealthy individuals.

Investors such as that will not take just anyone's call and agree to a meeting to hear a pitch. They respond to credibility and a track record. They require reasonable assurance that their principal will remain intact along with an excellent return on their investment. In order to have that reassurance, they will want some control such as a seat on the board of directors. It is normal for a successful capital raise to be comprised of a patchwork of deals in which investors pledge money in exchange for varying commitments (seats on the board of directors, high-level positions, etc.) from the founders.

The public relations task was to demonstrate credibility for the capital raise effort. Fortunately, the founders had done this successfully before. As a result of previous successful startups, the CEO had been nominated three times for the honor of the Ernst and Young *Entrepreneur of the Year*. Additionally, he was often called to testify before the U.S. Senate and House of Representatives on the impact of legislation on the financial services industry.

The president of the company had also participated in these ventures. Additionally, he had earned an MBA, law degree, PhD, and is an able man of the world who speaks five languages and serves as an adjunct law professor. He is familiar with jurisdictions and customs around the globe where the company seeks to establish markets.

The CEO, president, COO (chief operating officer) and wealth management managing director had operated together successfully for years. They had all played roles in the prior ventures.

The business model was complex. The bank would be chartered in Panama (avoiding the U.S. Dodd-Frank regulations and Federal Deposit Insurance Corporation or FDIC guidelines on lending). At the time, the banking system and economy were in the midst of a serious downturn that had resulted in multiple bank failures, so the regulatory environment in the U.S. was unfavorable. There would be an electronic foreign-currency exchange, a commercial finance company, and a U.S.-regulated broker-dealer. The funds available for commercial finance would come from deposits made in the international bank. The holding company would be based in Florida.

It is necessary to make the complex as simple as possible for public consumption, even for sophisticated investors.

For a variety of reasons, the founders were hesitant to pursue media coverage. As a regulated broker-dealer and investment company, there are a variety of compliance concerns to account for when talking to the public. Websites and brochures are considered "advertising" and various disclosures warning the investing public of the risks of investing must be provided. So is social media, and since we use websites and social media for press releases, we had to be careful of what is there. Also, projected investment performance cannot be stated or implied.

There is more to it, but compliance concerns often lend a vanilla, sanitized tone to public communication regarding investments and investment firms. Regulators of all jurisdictions scrutinize the media every day for stories about investment firms and licensed investment professionals.

Nonetheless, we decided together to pursue some media opportunities on a limited basis. To figure out where to start, I did not need to look far. There were framed newspaper articles and magazine covers on walls all around the office about the CEO. They would not be there if he did not like them, so those were excellent clues as to what sort of coverage he preferred and in what publications.

I developed a media plan to contact regional and statewide business publications, followed by national media (such as CNBC, the network that provides live, real time coverage of financial markets and business news). We wanted to gain the attention of investors around the world, so we included international business publications in the plan. We also developed some talking points, which were carefully coordinated to account for legal and compliance considerations.

I contacted the *Tampa Bay Times*. Formerly the *St. Petersburg Times*, the paper has a daily circulation of just over 400,000 (in 2011, according to Audit Bureau of Circulations) and is one of the most widely-read newspapers in Florida. Additionally, the company headquarters was located in the market of this newspaper. I read the business section in order to become familiar with the reporters and what they normally covered.

If you are going to successfully present stories to media, you must take some time to familiarize yourself with media. Find the right publication, the right site, the right TV show, etc.

The common approach is an indiscriminate blast faxed or e-mailed press release. You can certainly do that. But stop for a moment. Imagine picking up tomorrow's mail.

If you are like most people, you probably have a lot of direct mail advertising. There will be flyers, circulars, coupons, and "junk mail" in general. At election season it is even worse because of the constant flood of campaign literature.

Your e-mail inbox is probably even worse. How much spam do you get in any given day?

The blast press release is just junk mail and spam in the newsroom. It is poorly targeted and like direct mail campaigns, may get a 1% conversion rate. In other words, companies that market that way sell to 1% of their market and annoy the other 99%. The blast release is comparable. This approach is near the bottom of my list of preferred tactics.

To start this properly, I needed a reporter who was balanced, could grasp the details of this business, and was maybe even a bit of a skeptic. I found one and sent him a personalized e-mail. Later, I followed up with a phone call.

He took my call and listened to me. He was familiar with local banks and financial services firms and our founders, and agreed to write a feature story.

As always, I asked him what questions he wanted answered so that everyone could prepare. "In what direction would you like to take the interview?"

He wanted an overview of the concept, and how the experience of the founders' previous ventures prepared them for this new company. He wanted to know how it would work. He would ask why the bank would be chartered in Panama. He wanted to know about the local impact of the new company (number of jobs created, contracts, money lent, etc.).

We set a date for the interview and the *Tampa Bay Times* sent a photographer to take pictures of the CEO and president in advance.

The interview took place via conference call. The reporter never really deviated from the line of questioning that he had provided in advance, and completely understood the business model. Four days later, the story appeared in the business section of the Sunday edition of the *Tampa Bay Times*.

The CEO was quite happy about the article. The president took issue with one sentence, "...will be able to conduct banking activities that otherwise would not be permitted in the U.S."

We were referring to the bank in Panama and the freedom of not being subjected to FDIC regulation and the freedom from U.S. lending regulations. However, the president was also an attorney and was in the legal watchdog role for the company. To him, it looked like the article was hinting that the Panama bank could take deposits from anyone, anywhere in the world, no questions asked. That was not the case and he did not want it to appear that way (banks in Panama cannot accept deposits from proceeds of activity that violates international law, such as terrorism or narcotics).

The founders were very sensitive to such a perception. By the way, Panamanian banking regulators are too. After all, the holding company was in Florida with a regulated broker-dealer, easily within the reach of U.S. authorities. No company that was setting up to violate U.S. law would do that. The president made sure that he maintained open communication with regulators everywhere.

The CEO told me that the article resulted in investor interest of over $1 million.

Keys to Triumph

1. The founders had the credibility. It was just a matter of finding the right place and time to tell the story.

2. The founders made themselves accessible to this reporter. At the conclusion of the interview, they offered their personal cell phone numbers to him. Also, they were proactive with regulators. If you are in a regulated business, don't ever hide from regulators unless you want to create the impression that you are hiding something. The president was transparent to them and to the media. To look clean, be clean.

   If regulators take action against you, the media will know. If that happens, your business will experience a crisis on the regulatory AND the public fronts. Head that off with the sort of transparency that the president of this company showed, and by sound practices that stay within the law.

3. We took a sharpshooter approach to gaining media attention. This story was not something that just any reporter could cover. We chose carefully, and a good story seemed to just "fall into place." In reality, everybody was carefully prepared and well-suited.

Chapter 29 How it pays to get noticed: measuring return on investment from public relations.

Every business owner is oriented toward the bottom line to one extent or another. I often hear concerns from business owners about public relations and return on investment (ROI).

"If we do this, how is it going to affect my bottom line?"

Determining ROI is not an exact science. There are no guarantees that media coverage resulting from public relations (PR) will boost sales, and it is rarely possible to trace sales directly to PR efforts or a news story.

There is no guarantee that negative coverage will decrease sales either. In spite of consistent bad press that Wal-Mart receives about low wages paid to associates, their store traffic, sales, and revenue remain relatively stable.

PR is your best weapon to array the power of the media in the service of boosting your profile on your terms.

PR can enhance your reputation. Your reputation can increase traffic to your website, where website visits can drive sales. PR serves in a supporting role for the sales effort.

PR can also prevent disasters. *If you have bad news, what is it worth to you to keep you out of the spotlight?* The value of that cannot be measured.

PR can mitigate disasters. If you experience negative coverage, what is it worth to you to rehabilitate your public reputation? Again, that is hard to measure, but at least the baseline is easy to identify...it is when and where the negative coverage occurred. That should be where you see improvement and a turnaround if the PR is effective.

Here are some metrics:

-AVE-It has been common practice to measure PR using *Advertising Value Equivalency* (AVE). This is what a story would cost if it were advertising space or time. To calculate it for one month, measure column inches of space in a newspaper. Measure time occupied by a clip on TV or in radio. Then, just multiply the column inches by the advertising rate, or the time on TV or radio by the advertising rate. So, it measures length of coverage and volume of coverage. However, AVE is really an oversimplification.

AVE leads people to incorrectly assume that they can measure profitability by showing "dollar value" of publicity. It does not account for the quality of the story. A positive story is worth much more than an advertisement, and AVE can't measure that.

-Analytics-You can track analytics on your website and glean much from what the traffic data tells you where did it come from, where it goes, and what landing pages lead to orders and sales. Reading analytics is a good way of tracking activity within your website. Your website is a form of media that is within your control, so you can make changes with relative ease.

-Social media-PR efforts can be measured through social media. You can set a baseline, conduct a campaign through social media and measure "likes," followers, comments, and other levels of social engagement. Again, your social media is within your control, so you can make changes at will. The changes should be made based on trends in consumer opinion and desired content or features. When evaluating views, likes, etc., just know that there are peak times and days for Facebook use. For example, you will get fewer people seeing posts on a Sunday afternoon then you would on a Thursday afternoon. If you post something at 2 AM on a Monday, it is unlikely to get much visibility.

Social media networks can provide the most accurate data on peak times.

-Surveys-If the questions are formulated in a way to draw out responses in a way that is outcome-neutral, the results will be more trustworthy. Also, getting people to participate in a neutral way is challenging.

Start with a baseline. If you began a public relations campaign in January 2013 for example, sales or revenue may be associated with a PR campaign. From there, watch the impact of your campaign. You may be able to see some changes in these areas:

-ROI of media placements-Account for the demographics and circulation of publications where your stories are placed.
-ROI of search engine rankings. SEO is another part of a PR effort, and you may be able to see a difference in your rankings.
-ROI from analytics. Google changes algorithms from time to time, so the way it shares how traffic comes to your site may change. Do your best to keep up with Google changes for measuring both rankings and analytics.
-ROI from sales. One technique to measure effectiveness of a campaign is to devote a new URL (universal resource locator; a unique web address) directly and exclusively to that campaign, then measure traffic at that URL.

ROI from credibility may be the most important measure of all. It represents the real advantage of a PR investment over an investment in advertising.

The public relations firm Edelman conducts regular surveys on trust and credibility. In one recent survey, the question was simple. "I believe the information I get from articles and news stories more than the information I get from advertising." In the U.S., 86% agreed and in Europe, 83% agreed.

More than 35% in both the U.S. and Europe stated that "experts" such as academics or doctors who have no vested interest in the welfare of a company were the most trusted spokespersons. Fewer than 2 in 10 people said that paid representatives such as company spokespersons or athletes or entertainers are credible sources of information.

In the U.S. and Europe, information from independent parties is perceived to be far more credible sources (colleagues- 38%, friends and family-35%, and analyst's reports-26%) than information from corporate advertisements (5%) or websites (13%).

The bottom line is that the survey reported that, "the news media carries a high degree of credibility with opinion leaders, who are eight times more likely to believe information they receive from the news media than from advertising."

I repeat. People are eight times more likely to believe it if it came from the news than if it came from advertising.

Can we account for that in ROI for PR? Can we take the AVE and multiply it by 8 to get the real potential value of publicity?

Again, that is a rough number. I have heard another result of five times more credible. It depends on who is taking the survey. The results may not be completely consistent-- 8 to 1 is different than 5 to 1. However, the message IS consistent. *PR is far more credible than advertising.*

An advertisement is a company buying space to boast about itself. A media placement is a third party telling a story that concerns a company.

In *The Fall of Advertising and the Rise of PR* (Ries), the author argues that PR builds a brand and that advertising should defend the brand. He points out Starbucks as an example, spending less than $10 million on advertising in its first 10 years. Instead, it relied on word of mouth and a reputation for quality and a "hip" environment.

He also points to Volvo and their reputation for safety and quality. It was Volvo conducting safety tests, improving as a result, and then inviting third party safety institutes and engineers to conduct safety tests, with the press observing and publishing stories. They only bought advertising later. In this case, it worked. The advertising served to reaffirm the brand's credibility.

Advertising is a pitch and the only barrier between the advertiser and you in the newspaper is price. In contrast, PR has been filtered through an editor and a reporter in order to be deemed newsworthy.

Advertising is a flimsy way to mitigate bad news. For a real train wreck, look at what happened at Firestone after selling a line of defective tires. They ran advertisements in *The Wall Street Journal*, *The New York Times*, and *USA Today* that said, "Making it right." One could read that as, "we have made tires wrong for 50 years, got caught, and now we will start making them right."

Meanwhile, the company failed to put out a consistent message. One spokesperson gave the media the impression that if customers were unhappy about their tires that Firestone would replace them at no charge. When customers tried to do that, they were told that would be required to pay a prorated fee for new tires. In a PR disaster that dwarfed the insincerity of the ad, Firestone had to issue a clarification press release.

PR is credible, but the company itself must be credible. We can talk all day about measuring effectiveness of PR and ROI of PR, but in the end the company cannot mask bad practices. All things being normal, ROI can be measured to some extent, but never exactly.

The metrics are important, but credibility is what sets PR apart as an investment.

Chapter 30 How to raise your profile from nothing at all...fast and cheap!

You have started a business, or something that passes for one. You have built it to a point where you just might be ready to make a sale as soon as a customer materializes from somewhere. It is not perfect, it needs development, but you can work with it.

If so, this is a good time to start some public relations work. To pull this off you will need to combine the old ways with the new ways. That means SEO combined with the classic public relations methods of garnering favorable press coverage. *SEO IS PR*.

Use SEO to build a foundation. To do this, you will first need a website, a phone number and an address for your business. You are starting to get your name out there, so make sure you can be located. Don't market something that is not there yet.

The Plan

This plan is simple and inexpensive but labor intensive. You are going to create an online presence with social media and by registering in online directories.

Social Media

Set up profiles in LinkedIn, Facebook, Twitter, YouTube, Blogger, Pinterest, and others. The beauty of social media is that the content is within your control, as it is with your website and blog. Set them up well and start gaining "likes" and followers. Ask your friends to participate. It will not take long before you see supporters, influencers and cheerleaders emerge. Be sure to reciprocate whenever possible.

Blogs

If you write blogs, link them to your website and social media. You are writing blog articles for two reasons. One, you want to contribute to the knowledge bank of your customers and be a resource. Two, you are getting an SEO benefit from it when you incorporate relevant keywords and links (ask other businesses to link to your site too, but be selective).

Here are some guidelines to help you write strong articles:

1. Avoid writing in ways that are entirely focused on your business or industry. Are you in title insurance? I am sorry to break this to you, but nobody cares about "Latest Best Practices in the Title Insurance Industry." Instead, write about how someone can use or profit from your product or service. Focus outward. How does what you do add value to your clients? If you are writing to add value to someone else's life, you are on the right path. If you are simply "you"-centric, few will read it. To be interesting, be interested.

2. Take time to research keywords that are *relevant to your prospective customers*. Think of what keywords *they* use to find someone who solves the problems that you solve. Include those keywords throughout your article so that you gain organic (unpaid) SEO.

3. You will not connect with all of your readers. Don't bother watering it down and trying to make it "safe". The ones who you do connect with will believe in you and will tell your story for you.

4. Humanize it. Don't sanitize it. If you own the business, you only need to answer to yourself so be yourself. Write with as much verve and panache as you can. Put soul into your writing.

5. If you are writing about something controversial, have an opinion and own it. Challenge readers to see it your way. Be

thought-provoking. If you have offended someone, you may be doing something right.

6. Use proper English, grammar, punctuation and spelling. Get another set of eyes on it whenever possible. Also, step away from it for a while after you have finished writing it. Take another look at it after some time has passed; it will look different. That is a good time to edit or add polish. Once you are satisfied, go ahead and publish it.

7. Write a strong headline. You will find that writing a good headline can be challenging sometimes. Again, you want to talk to a latent need of your reader, not blow your own horn. Sum up what is best and most relevant about your article. You have one sentence to do this.

Social media and blogs are great weapons for an early-stage entrepreneur. They certainly provide cost-effective ways to get noticed on your terms. However, they also offer you a chance to sell your idea your way. You started a business for a reason. You took this risk for a reason. You forsook the security of a regular corporate paycheck for a reason. You want to do it your way and are now offering your concept, your service, or your product to the people of your market. Offer it with pride and confidence.

Online Directories

Now that you have a website, a blog, and a social media presence, it is time to register in some online directories. These directories have a great deal of traffic, so linking to them will help some customers find you and add SEO strength.

This will be time-consuming, but worth it. These directories are currently free. They are currently leading online directories. You can register your business with them at no charge. Expect phone calls and upgrade offers, but you do not need paid listings to get the SEO benefits.

1. Google+
2. Bing Business
3. Yahoo Local
4. YellowPages.com
5. Superpages.com
6. MerchantCircle
7. Citysearch (CityGrid)
8. InsiderPages
9. Foursquare
10. TripAdvisor

After you have done this, it may take a couple of weeks or so to see the registrations show up in the search engines. You will notice that your business has risen in the rankings.

Reputation Management

Your online reputation is a collection of mentions and reviews about you and your company on the World Wide Web. There are some sites that provide monitoring, and you can register with them in order to receive alerts when new items regarding you or your business appear in the search engines.

1. Google Alerts
2. Naymz
3. Tweet Beep
4. Social Mention
5. Monitor This

Smartphone proliferation presents some hazards.

Customers can easily leave reviews. People will submit reviews at the height of emotion. If someone visits a medical office for an appointment and receives rude treatment from a receptionist or their appointment starts late, that person may leave a bad review while sitting in the waiting area. If someone has a bad experience at a restaurant that ruins an evening, they can review it right then and there on the phone.

It takes effort and expense to overcome the effects of these reviews. Reputation management firms can help overcome bad reviews, adverse regulatory filings that make it into search engines, or other events that affect your online reputation. Think Big Enterprises of Tampa, FL is one such firm, and they have protocols which can be customized for clients.

Such protocols involve detailed mitigation and repair, which normally involve content campaigns and ongoing monitoring.

Google currently rewards businesses handsomely with over five reviews of four or five stars. Just as positive media can be earned, positive reviews can be too. However, they must be genuine. States are cracking down on rigged reviews and passing laws to prevent them.

So, that is the plan. In summary, you build a foundation of online presence with social media, blogs, and registration in online directories. Reputation management serves as a guard. All of this can be done within a couple of weeks, and most of it is free.

Once this foundation is in place, take your PR efforts to the next level by looking for opportunities to obtain press coverage. It should be as big as possible. If you can gain positive coverage in a well-respected media outlet with a large circulation or audience, the SEO benefits are significant and lasting.

Now What?

If you are starting a business and want to publicize it, keep this book nearby. If you are established, keep it nearby anyway because the fundamentals are here in these pages.

Isolate what is different about you and gear your life toward honoring that difference. Getting noticed on your terms means that your world recognizes and celebrates that strength and difference with you.

That is a public triumph!

ABOUT THE AUTHOR

James Chittenden founded Triumph Business Communications which provides clients with a full range of public relations services. James was a Marine Corps officer before spending nearly a decade in business in securities and business banking.

In addition to Triumph Business Communications, he also founded Triumph Business Services, which provides incorporation services to entrepreneurs.

As a Marine Corps officer, he led high-visibility, high-traffic public affairs efforts in times of war and peace.

In addition to publishing a base newspaper, he has served as a spokesperson on countless occasions. He has helped others to develop their own latent abilities to do so as well, from young recruits to generals to employees and CEOs.

James graduated from Florida State University where he studied history and economics, and earned a Master's Degree in Business Administration from Boston University. Additionally, he is a graduate of the Defense Information School in Ft. Meade, MD, where he studied journalism and public affairs.

James M. Chittenden